Praise for *The Economics of Higher Purpose*

"Quinn and Thakor create a powerful case and practical guide for why and how we should run into a burning building. Their eight counterintuitive steps for purpose-driven management are a must-read for leaders who understand that all you can command is attendance, and all the good stuff is given willingly by those that understand and share the higher purpose of their organization."
  —**Jim Mallozzi, former Chairman and CEO, Prudential Real Estate and Relocation Services**

"As an HR leader, I am constantly thinking about how to provide a richer, more meaningful work experience. *The Economics of Higher Purpose* provides a compelling blueprint to help our people connect to a deeper purpose in their work. If this is done well, work becomes more than a paycheck; it satisfies our desire to be a part of something bigger."
  —**Shawn P. Patterson, Vice President of Organizational Effectiveness and Chief Learning Officer, DTE Energy**

"In this book, Quinn and Thakor teach us a great yet challenging lesson: when we learn to look beyond profit maximization to a higher purpose, we learn to create lasting prosperity."
  —**Charles C. Manz, Nirenberg Chaired Professor of Leadership, University of Massachusetts Amherst, and coauthor of *Twisted Leadership* and *Twisted Teams***

"In their new book, Quinn and Thakor share amazing insights and stories on how higher purpose turns everyone into a fully invested person. This volume is a profound playbook for those who want to unleash the human and economic power in the people around them."
  —**Jim Haudan, Chairman, Root Inc.**

"The authors take us on a compelling journey in which we discover the why and the how of creating organizations of higher purpose. Then they give us the gift of practical tools and exercises—it is a precious volume for those who want to make a difference."
  —**Nick Craig, author of *Leading from Purpose***

"By discovering what has made some organizations so hugely successful, Thakor and Quinn give higher purpose the instrumental role it deserves in everybody's life project, large or small. They have written a fantastic, eye-opening book. It is both visionary and highly practical. I have followed their rules unknowingly for the better part of my life."
  —**Jan Krahnen, Professor of Finance, Goethe University, and Founding Director, Sustainable Architecture for Finance in Europe**

"Everyone has a brand. This book will teach you how to translate your purpose, vision, and values into a strong personal and professional brand. The book leads you on a journey that will help you understand the power of your personal brand and nurture its evolution throughout your career."

—**Dave Ulrich, Rensis Likert Professor, Ross School of Business, University of Michigan, and Partner, The RBL Group**

The Economics
of
Higher Purpose

Eight Counterintuitive Steps for Creating a Purpose-Driven Organization

ROBERT E. QUINN
ANJAN V. THAKOR

BK

Berrett–Koehler Publishers, Inc.

Berrett-Koehler Publishers, Inc.
1333 Broadway, Suite 1000
Oakland, CA 94612-1921
Tel: (510) 817-2277
Fax: (510) 817-2278
www.bkconnection.com

ORDERING INFORMATION
Quantity sales. Special discounts are available on quantity purchases by corporations, associations, and others. For details, contact the "Special Sales Department" at the Berrett-Koehler address above.
Individual sales. Berrett-Koehler publications are available through most bookstores. They can also be ordered directly from Berrett-Koehler: Tel: (800) 929-2929; Fax: (802) 864-7626; www.bkconnection.com.
Orders for college textbook/course adoption use. Please contact Berrett-Koehler: Tel: (800) 929-2929; Fax: (802) 864-7626.

Distributed to the US trade and internationally by Penguin Random House Publisher Services.

Berrett-Koehler and the BK logo are registered trademarks of Berrett-Koehler Publishers, Inc.

Printed in Canada

Berrett-Koehler books are printed on long-lasting acid-free paper. When it is available, we choose paper that has been manufactured by environmentally responsible processes. These may include using trees grown in sustainable forests, incorporating recycled paper, minimizing chlorine in bleaching, or recycling the energy produced at the paper mill.

Library of Congress Cataloging-in-Publication Data

Names: Quinn, Robert E., author. | Thakor, Anjan., author.
Title: The economics of higher purpose : eight counterintuitive steps for creating a purpose-
    driven organization / Robert E. Quinn, Anjan V. Thakor.
Description: First Edition. | Oakland, CA : Berrett-Koehler Publishers, 2019.
Identifiers: LCCN 2019007916 | ISBN 9781523086405 (hardback)
Subjects: LCSH: Organizational behavior. | Employee motivation. | Work environment. | BISAC:
    BUSINESS & ECONOMICS / Organizational Behavior. | BUSINESS & ECONOMICS /
    Workplace Culture. | BUSINESS & ECONOMICS / Motivational.
Classification: LCC HD58.7 .Q5586 2019 | DDC 658—dc23
LC record available at https://lccn.loc.gov/2019007916

First Edition

27 26 25 24 23 22 21 20 19 | 10 9 8 7 6 5 4 3 2 1

Book producer and text designer: BookMatters, Berkeley
Cover designer: Leslie Waltzer, Crowfoot Design
Copyeditor: Mike Mollett; Proofer: Janet Reed Blake; Indexer: Leonard Rosenbaum

CONTENTS

PREFACE

Professors of management and professors of finance speak two different languages, so communication among them is very limited. The two of us, Bob and Anjan, not only talk, we cherish talking. We cherish it because we have a higher purpose. We love learning, and we both yearn to help others gain the love of learning. When we talk together, we not only move forward, we also flourish. We flourish because we have established such a high-quality connection that we make each other better. When we spend a day together, we spend weeks afterward unpacking all the new ideas.

For more than twenty years, we have traveled the globe together running workshops, making presentations, and interviewing senior executives. As we have had these rich experiences, each of us has always been incredibly interested in what the other thinks. We take an experience that captivates us on a given day. Then we collectively ponder it. We explore it from the perspective of management theory. Then we analyze it from the perspective of financial theory. Then we seek to integrate what we have learned. As we do this, we become bilingual as we learn to speak a little more of each other's professional language, and we take on a more inclusive mind-set in which differences can be integrated.

Since neither of us fully understands what the other is talking about, we have to pay close attention. We also have to reduce complex ideas down to notions with which the other can connect. We also have to become vulnerable. We have to expose our ignorance and confess that we do not understand. Since we both respect and trust each other, we are comfortable exposing our ignorance as we join in mutual exploration.

A relationship of purpose, trust, vulnerability, and learning often gives rise to new capacities. The capacities are real. There have been times when we have put together a major presentation, requiring the integration of complex concepts, in less than five minutes. If one of us did the same task with a different person, it would take days. We are able to do this because we live in a relationship based on trust, and trust gives rise to collective intelligence. Together, we can do extraordinary things.

The Birth of This Book

In 2006 Bob was asked to serve without pay for three years as president of a mission for the Church of Jesus Christ of Latter-Day Saints in Adelaide, Australia. So he and his wife, Delsa, went to Australia. In 2009 Anjan was to receive a major award in St. Louis, and Bob, who had just returned from the mission, flew to St. Louis to be at the awards ceremony. As soon as they were together, Anjan began inquiring about Bob's experience in Australia.

Bob described his efforts to build a positive organization driven by a higher purpose. As the people in the organization pursued the higher purpose, they became fully unified and engaged. They began to collaborate and learn in the same way that Anjan and Bob had collaborated and learned. The people had a sense of purpose, contribution, positivity, and growth, and the organization performed at a high level.

Anjan became engrossed in the account and asked one probing question after another until the conversation was interrupted. That night during a break in the ceremony, Anjan dashed across the room and grabbed Bob by the arm. He said, "Your story violates the assumptions of economics. Economics suggests that wealth is created by a single-minded focus on shareholder value or wealth maximization. There is no place for higher purpose or for positive culture in the logic of value creation. You must choose one or the other. We need to write a paper. In the morning we should meet before you fly out."

That meeting and the discussion eventually grew into a research project. We built a mathematical model of an organization. The model was composed of principals (bosses) and agents (employees) engaged in conventional relationships of transactional exchange: for this amount of money, we agree that you will do this amount of work.

We then altered the model. We introduced a collective purpose higher than profit. When we introduced the higher purpose, the organization was transformed. The employees began to act like owners. The assumptions of self-interested, transactional exchange fell away. The employees became intrinsically motivated and were willing to go the extra mile to reach their goals. The model was an organization of higher purpose.

In interpreting our findings, we concluded that, on the one hand, value creation and the pursuit of higher purpose can conflict with profit maximization as conventionally understood. Yet, on the other hand, value creation and purpose can also be complementary. We began to focus on the notion that some leaders learn to transcend fear and intellectual arrogance. They begin to integrate the seemingly conflicting assumptions of management and of economics, and this results in a more inclusive mind-set. They create an economy of higher purpose and begin to more fully tap the potential of a given organization.

We desired to find out more about how real leaders imbue organizations with purpose and create economies in which people thrive and exceed expectations. We assumed the heads of organizations would understand this notion, so we began by interviewing more than 25 leaders who were known for having organizations of higher purpose. Some were from Fortune 500 companies. Some were from entrepreneurial companies. Some were from outside the business world.

The interviews generated a surprising finding. Some of the CEOs did not believe in purpose when they first became CEOs. They were steeped in the conventional perspective of economics, and they were blinded by intellectual arrogance. They saw no value in purpose as a transformer of people and culture. The notion of discovering, articulating, and clarifying higher purpose seemed like a wasteful distraction.

They discovered the power of purpose only as a result of some traumatic challenge. When they were challenged in that way, they experienced deep learning. The conventional approaches they used to lead their organizations seemed ineffective in handling the major challenges they were confronting. They needed to turn to something unconventional, something transformative. Many found the answer in an authentic higher purpose for their organization.

Consequently, these leaders evolved from a narrow to an inclusive mind-set. This mind-set allowed them to incorporate higher purpose and positive organizing. They became "bilingual leaders" who could converse in both the language of transactional problem solving and the contributive language of higher purpose.

This allowed them to appreciate the reality of constraints, without losing sight of the reality of possibilities. They could recognize, surface, and transform conflict—which tightens constraints—into creative collaboration that expanded possibilities. They could elevate the collective intelligence and create cultures where people flourished and exceeded expectations.

As we continued to interview purpose-driven people, teach classes, run workshops, and help executives change their organizations, we constantly explored the notion of higher purpose, positive culture, and bilingual capacity. We became increasingly clear in our belief that there were two worldviews that needed to be integrated.

Higher Purpose

This book is about how to create an organization of higher purpose. An organization of higher purpose is a social system in which the greater good has been envisioned, articulated, and authenticated. Like all organizations, an organization of higher purpose is a cauldron of conflict. Yet the higher purpose is the arbiter of all decisions, and people find meaning in their work and in their relationships despite the conflicts. They share a vision and are fully engaged. They strive to transcend their egos and sacrifice for the common good.

In an organization of higher purpose, despite constant pressures to regress to the norm, the people interact with one another with respect and engage in constructive confrontation. Trust is continually repaired, and conversations are authentic. The people have a win-win mentality, and positive peer pressure emerges to support high levels of collaboration. They maintain these collaborative relationships in the face of recurring adversity. Leadership not only flows from the top down, but it also emerges from the bottom up. Meetings are generative, and members of the organization co-create the future. Employees believe they work in an organization of excellence. Customers and other external constituents are drawn to the excellence and confirm it by joining in the co-creation of the organization's future.

The Organization of the Book

This book is organized into two parts, and you may prefer to read either or both. Part 1 examines the theories that govern organizational behavior, some of which are also formally articulated in economics. We believe these conventional assumptions of economics are valid but incomplete. Hence, we offer a new logic that transcends the conventional assumptions and includes them. We show that higher purpose helps to resolve the classic principal–agent problem at the heart of microeconomics. We explain why numerous books and articles on higher purpose have failed to gain traction in the workplace.

In part 2, we shift from theory to practice. We offer a framework of eight counterintuitive guidelines, which are drawn from research and from our interviews with leaders of higher-purpose organizations.

Each chapter explains one guideline and shows why it is counterintuitive and often ignored. We offer grounded illustrations of how the guidelines can be understood and implemented. The guidelines provide a way for you to find your organization's higher purpose and a way to intersect the purpose with the organization's strategy. We conclude each chapter with an exercise you can do to begin the journey to finding your own higher purpose. In the final chapter, we list and answer the practical questions of many executives, and we provide some advice on how to get started.

PART I

The Economics of Higher Purpose

Part I, chapters 1 through 6, describes the economics of higher purpose. In chapter 1 we present an overview of the book. We discuss how conventional assumptions prevent us from recognizing the impact of higher purpose in people and in organizations. In chapter 2 we show that higher purpose changes everything. We give illustrations of how embracing higher purpose transforms human potential at both the individual and organizational levels, and we review the research verifying the impacts of higher purpose. In chapter 3 we suggest that it is difficult for professionals to imagine organizations of higher purpose. Conventional thinking is based on bipolar logic that values knowing over learning. We explain the need for an economic logic based on assumptions of inclusion, of learning, and of growth.

In chapter 4 we review the central framework of microeconomics, the principal agent model. This model describes how relationships ought to be structured between principals (owners of productive assets) and agents (those who work for the principals). It starts with the assumption that self-interest causes the goals of the principal and agent to diverge, and it seeks to design contracts to minimize the misalignment of incentives resulting from the pursuit of self-interest. We suggest that this model, which normally predicts behavior so well, is based on assumptions that diminish the ability of leaders to inspire behavior that results in organizations of exceptional performance.

In chapter 5 we discuss turning everyone into a fully invested person. We elaborate on the principal–agent model and suggest that the mentality of contracts must be supplanted by the mentality of covenants. Leaders can create purpose-driven organizations in which people exceed expectations. Finally, because executives, for sound reasons, avoid working on higher purpose, we suggest that you have a golden opportunity. Chapter 6 explains why so many leaders avoid purpose work. We address the question "Why isn't everyone doing it?"

By understanding the economics of higher purpose and internalizing the principles in part 2, you can become a person who creates a purpose-driven organization.

CHAPTER ONE

Seeing What Cannot Be Seen

Economics is a rigorous field that is concerned with the study of economic exchange and the resulting economic output. It studies the markets in which economic exchange occurs. It studies the entrepreneurs and organizations that produce the output involved in these economic exchanges, as well as the employees who work in the organizations. And it seeks to understand the behavior of the households that consume the economic output. Economics pays little, if any, attention to how the very purpose of organizations— their reason to exist—guides their decisions. Often, this purpose is stated in the language of economic output—banks exist to safeguard depositors' money and lend to borrowers, automobile companies exist to make and sell cars, and so forth. That is, purpose is stated in the context of *business purpose.*

In this book, we look beyond business purpose to *higher purpose.* Higher purpose is a prosocial goal that is defined not in terms of economic output but in terms of the contribution the organization makes to society. So when Starbucks states its reason for being as providing its customers "a third place between work and home " it is articulating a higher purpose that transcends its business goals but yet intersects with them.

Higher purpose can be pursued by all organizations, big and small, and at every level within the organization. But the pursuit of higher purpose is not the norm. Rather, it is an *exception* to the norm, so you will not find it when you look at the average organization. Micah Solomon gives the following example, quoting Jay Coldren in this story about The Inn at Little Washington in Washington, Virginia. This is something Coldren observed on his first day on the job at the hotel:

> I watched a couple arrive at The Inn from Pittsburgh, several hours away, to celebrate their anniversary with a three-night stay. As the staff unloaded the luggage, our female guest said to her husband, "Don't forget my hanging bag." Her husband looked into the trunk and came up with a horrified expression on his face. Apparently, she had left her bag beside the car in their garage assuming he would pack it, but he never saw it.
>
> At this point, she pretty much fell apart: This poor woman was checking into one of the most expensive places on the planet with nothing but the clothes on her back! As the doormen and I tried to figure out what to do to make this couple happy, one of the staff who had been there a lot longer than me drove up to the front of the inn in the company car. I looked at him oddly and he just smiled and said, "Get me their keys and the address; I'll be back before dinner."
>
> I was floored. No one asked him to do this, and there wasn't a moment's hesitation on his part. He was so much a part of the service culture that he just knew the exact right thing to do. He was halfway to Pittsburgh before the lady actually believed that we were really going to get her luggage at her house. He drove eight hours straight and made it back before their dinner reservations at nine.[1]

This is an example of a purpose-driven employee. Instead of minimizing effort like a typical "agent," he took ownership. The fact that people like him exist is important. When we're coaching executives on how to do purpose work in their organizations, we often tell them to do something paradoxical—look not for typical behavior as reflected in large-sample averages, but look for exceptions. These are the outliers. Look for excellence via positive deviance, examine the purpose that drives the excellence, and then imagine your entire workforce imbued with that purpose. But purpose work is not meant to be charity. Rather, it is about behavior that is woven into the fabric of your business model.

This book is all about the unique *intersection* between business practice and higher purpose.

Economics teaches us that people tend to be self-interested and effort averse. Managers often say, "My people do not work as hard as I do unless they are paid enough, and even then I have to watch over them."

This work-resistant logic drives managers to create systems of control. Employees recognize that the control systems are in place, and they often respond by devising ways to circumvent the control and blunt its effectiveness. This behavior reconfirms the initial assumptions of the manager and demonstrates a need for more control. Over time the employees become less engaged, and the manager becomes more frustrated.

The surprising truth is that when managers accept the empirically sound assumptions of economics and related disciplines that employees are effort averse and work hard only if sufficiently monitored and compensated, these gloomy assumptions become self-fulfilling prophecies, and the workforce tends to underperform. Energy is dissipated, output is sacrificed, and there is no logical way out of the energy-draining vicious cycle.

But there is an alternative view of organizational behavior, a view in which the organization gains an authentic, prosocial, higher purpose that transcends the usual business goals and affects decisions big and small. When this view takes hold, the collective interest becomes the self-interest and employees become less work resistant. It happens because a paradoxical shift is created. When employees make the shift, they begin to see things that cannot normally be seen.

From Transaction to Contribution

Managers often make well-justified, negative assumptions about employees and then design systems that end up bringing forth the assumed negative behaviors. They must transform the vicious cycle into a virtuous, self-reinforcing cycle. To do this, they have to shift the transaction-oriented mind that is focused on constraints to the purpose-motivated mind that is focused on the service of possibility. They enter the realm of imagination and emotion, and there they clarify a passionate, higher purpose that orbits around contribution.

When managers become purpose driven, they begin to transform into leaders. They begin to transcend conventional thinking, and they begin to comprehend the economics of higher purpose. They come to understand that when an authentic higher purpose permeates business strategy and decision making, the personal good and the collective good become one, and the vicious cycle is broken. Both employers and employees begin to engage more fully. They collaborate and exceed expectations. Long-term economic benefits are produced.

This works, however, only if employees believe that the higher purpose is authentic. If higher purpose is pursued solely for economic gain, it will be viewed as a tool of manipulation, and employees will recognize it immediately. They will see it as one more attempt to control, and it may fail to produce long-term economic gains. Unless the higher purpose becomes the arbiter of every strategy and leadership decision, the organization has no higher purpose. Herein lies the paradox: an authentic organizational higher purpose will change the fundamental implicit contract between employers and employees and change behavior, thereby producing long-term economic gain, but *only if it is not pursued with the intent of producing economic gain.*

Why Is the Pursuit of Higher Purpose Not More Common?

At this stage, we often find that people have questions like these: This sounds good, but if it is such a great idea, why isn't everyone doing it?

This question is natural, and chapter 6 is devoted to answering it. But for now we note that managers often reject the option to pursue higher purpose based in part on their level in the organization— many feel they are not high enough in the organization to implement organizational change. Think of the CEO's choice. Some of the reasons why CEOs do not pursue higher purpose are these:

➢ Lack of belief and personal doubt. Many leaders think of their workforce as being self-interested and motivated only by additional wealth, organizational prestige, and promotions. Thus, they view the pursuit of higher purpose as not being in their best business interest, and they think that a serious embrace of higher purpose will cost the organization in terms of business outcomes.

➢ The tyranny of the here and now. How do I pursue higher purpose when I barely have time for the next crisis? Time is precious and scarce. Many CEOs feel that they do not have the luxury of time to pursue higher purpose.

➢ What will my financiers think? Pursuit of higher purpose may sometimes be difficult for shareholders and creditors to distinguish from the pursuit of pet projects that provide personal benefits to the CEO at the expense of shareholder wealth. This misgiving may make them suspicious of the CEO embracing higher purpose and devoting organizational resources to it.

➢ Cultural disconnect. How do I promote collaboration around the pursuit of higher purpose in an organization that does not value it? How can higher purpose have positive impact in an organization with a control- and competition-focused culture?

How to Do It: The Path to Organizational Higher Purpose

These barriers notwithstanding, we provide a practical eight-step process to help you discover your organization's higher purpose and successfully imbue the organization with it:

Step 1: Envision the Purpose-Driven Organization

A major impediment to the adoption of organizational higher purpose is that the organization's leaders do not really believe in it, as we discussed in the preface. Because they view their employees as being rational, self-interested economic agents, they believe that the employees cannot become a purpose-driven workforce. Nonetheless, they perceive pressure to come up with a statement of purpose. So they create a task force or hire public relations (PR) consultants to help them. They come up with a statement that is presented to the organization and the outside world, but the statement does not change the organization's decisions or its people. So the first step in the process is that you change your mind-set to envision a purpose-driven workforce. If you don't believe it, you will never see its value.

Step 2: Discover the Purpose

Once you have altered your mind-set and accepted the notion of a purpose-driven workforce, the next step is to articulate a higher purpose. A striking fact that we discovered in our research is that a purpose is not invented. It is discovered. It is already there, latent and invisible to most, but it is there nonetheless. It is currently embedded in both the feelings and the thoughts of the people. The leader's job is to help the organization discover it. While discovering it may take some time, the correct perspective is to view this step not as a wasteful expenditure of time but as an important investment in the future of the organization.

Step 3: Meet the Need for Authenticity

The higher purpose that you discover must meet a crucial test—it must be authentic. Perhaps the most important finding of our research is the importance of authenticity of organizational purpose. If purpose is a PR gimmick, a slogan put up on the walls, employees see through it. They become cynical. If the higher purpose is not authentic, it may do more harm than good. We will show you how to avoid this and create an authentic purpose message in which the people believe and invest. Authenticity also ensures that higher purpose will change the culture of the organization from one of intrafirm competition and conflict to one of shared beliefs, renewed commitment to the purpose, and cooperation. This change in culture will reduce self-interested behavior within the organization. So down the road it will actually free up time and enable greater focus on exceeding the customer's expectations and less on resolving organizational conflicts.

Step 4: Turn the Higher Purpose into a Constant Arbiter

Having discovered and articulated an authentic higher purpose, you must turn your attention to communicating it. When we are helping organizations implement a higher purpose, we are sometimes asked, "When will we be done?" What we have found is that the organization is never done. Higher purpose is a journey, not a destination. So it is really important for leaders to constantly and clearly communicate the higher purpose and to reinforce it by letting the organization know how its higher purpose has affected its business decisions. We show you how to turn purpose into a constant message, the arbiter of every decision, the driver of hard choices, and a differentiator for the organization. Such clear and constant communication can also serve as the basis for communicating purpose to the firm's financiers.

Step 5: Stimulate Learning

After you communicate higher purpose, you must follow up by stimulating employee learning that will facilitate the task of operationalizing the purpose within the organization. This step enables employees to use their creativity and smarts to come up with new ways to productively link their day-to-day decisions with the higher purpose of the organization. While we recognize the importance of the conventional focus on motivation by extrinsic rewards, we show you how higher purpose, by stimulating learning, also generates intrinsic, nonpecuniary rewards for employees. These can significantly enhance the power of extrinsic rewards.

Step 6: Turn Midlevel Managers into Purpose-Driven Leaders

Once you have discovered a higher purpose and articulated it, you must enlist midlevel managers to become purpose-driven leaders. Purpose cannot remain the responsibility of only those at the top—the task of leading must be spread throughout the ranks. While conventional management thinking views midlevel managers as responding to authority, we show you how to turn your midlevel managers into people who inspire through purpose, authenticity, and vulnerability.

Step 7: Connect the People to the Purpose

After you enlist the help of midlevel managers as purpose-driven leaders, you must seek to broaden the base of those who connect with the purpose. A key step in this process is to make sure the organizational higher purpose becomes personal for its employees. This means that you connect employees *emotionally* to the higher purpose so they become invested in it. While the role of positive emotion is not emphasized in conventional management thinking, we show you how to emotionally connect all the people to the purpose. The purpose must capture not only people's minds but also their hearts.

Step 8: Unleash the Positive Energizers

In every organization there are "positive energizers," those who exude positive energy that is infectious. These people are not risk averse. They are not effort averse. Everybody knows who they are. Leaders can tap this valuable off-balance-sheet resource and use these employees to be ambassadors for imbuing the organization with higher purpose. While it is commonly assumed that change is a top-down process, we show you how to unleash the positive energizers and initiate change at *every* level.

The eight steps suggest a progressive logic of actions that follow a sequence: envision a purpose-driven organization, discover the purpose, monitor for authenticity and constancy, stimulate collective learning, transform midlevel managers, connect to the workforce, and unleash the positive energizers. They can thus be used as a checklist. Yet you may begin to notice that the process is not as linear as you might wish. The process is full of recursive loops. It is about constantly acting, reflecting, learning, adapting, and acting again. To create a purpose-driven organization, you must reflect what you seek to create—you must be a purpose-driven person, willing to suffer learning because you live for the collective good.

An Anecdote and Definitions

In researching this book, we interviewed Richard (Dick) Mahoney, the former CEO of Monsanto. Dick was CEO at a time when Monsanto had chemicals divisions in its portfolio; these businesses were eventually divested. Dick told us about the time that they first began monitoring emissions of pollutants in 1987. Dick said he was shocked at Monsanto's numbers and decided that the company not only needed to improve but that it had to have such spectacularly low emission numbers that it would become an icon for the industry. He asked for a 90 percent reduction within six years. While many believed it could not be done, Dick said the surprising thing was how the goal energized the company around a worthwhile cause and created pride in the employees. The results were stunning, and they set the tone not only for Monsanto's conversations with the EPA but also for the industry as a whole. As his successor, Robert Shapiro, states,

> My predecessor, Dick Mahoney, understood that the way we were doing things had to change. Dick grew up, as I did not, in the chemical industry, so he tended to look at what was coming out of our plants. The publication of our first toxic-release inventory in 1988 galvanized attention around the magnitude of plant emissions.
>
> Dick got way out ahead of the traditional culture in Monsanto and in the rest of the chemical industry. He set incredibly aggressive quantitative targets and deadlines. The first reaction to them was, My God, he must be out of his mind. But it was an effective technique. In six years, we reduced our toxic air emissions by 90 percent.[2]

With his decision about what Monsanto would pursue after he looked at the company's emissions data, Dick Mahoney created an authentic higher purpose that had economic consequences. There are four key words: *economics, authentic, higher,* and *purpose.* These words seem simple and familiar. Yet when integrated, they create an image that is neither simple nor familiar. We now define each word, in reverse order.

Purpose: We tend to be path dependent.[3] In other words, the decisions we make in a given situation are highly shaped by the decisions we have made in the past. Generally, the past determines the present, and people tend to live in a reactive state.

Purpose is a proactive notion. Consider this unusual question: When does the future determine the present? The answer is, when we clarify and commit to an envisioned image. Dick Mahoney identified a future six years hence for Monsanto in which it had 90 percent lower emissions. That determined how the company behaved in the present. Purpose is an intention that creates focus and draws us into the creation of a new future.

Higher: Social scientists tell us that most of the time people are self-interested. People tend to be self-centered or egocentric. They seek what is best for them, often at the cost of what is best for others. They are oriented to compete for the acquisition of resources.

Higher means "loftier." A higher purpose refers to an intention that is grander than conventional self-interest. It reflects a desire to contribute, a hunger to serve some greater good. When Dick became wedded to the prosocial higher purpose of reducing emissions to help the environment, he altered conventional behavior at Monsanto. The collective interest of Monsanto and the personal interests of its employees converged because employees took personal pride in, and personal ownership of, the higher purpose. It was not just Dick's higher purpose. It was theirs! Therefore, a transformation occurred. People pulled together in the face of a challenge, and they produced an extraordinary outcome.

Authentic: Conventional assumptions make this word particularly difficult to access. Synonyms for authentic are *true, accurate, genuine, real, valid,* and *original.* Antonyms are *false* or *fake.* An authentic message is not fake; it is genuine. It transcends social expectations and comes unfiltered. We pay attention when we hear an authentic message because we do not expect to hear one. No one at Monsanto expected Dick Mahoney to set a goal of 90 percent emissions reduction in six years. It was an authentic message, not one shaped by narrow self-interest. An authentic message comes from an integrated heart and mind. At Monsanto it reflected the common desires and thoughts of the collective workforce and became the arbiter of every decision.

Economics: An authentic higher purpose is contributive. It is about contribution. Economics is conventionally about economic exchange: I give you something, and you give me something else in exchange. Having an authentic higher purpose means we contribute with no explicit expectation of getting something in return. That is, to be viewed as authentic, the pursuit of higher purpose must not be viewed as some sort of transactional exchange with employees, customers, and others—"We will do this for you today so you can do something for us tomorrow." Dick's articulation of higher purpose was not based on any expectation that employees would work harder and the stock price would go up or that the EPA would go easy on Monsanto in the future.

It is like giving a gift to a friend. If the friend knows you want a favor, the gift loses much of its meaning—it feels more like a bribe. The paradox then is that when a higher purpose is authentic—it is not being pursued explicitly for economic gain—and it is communicated with clarity, it actually produces economic gain! From a purely economic standpoint, however, since achieving such outcomes requires *no* up-front expectation of an economic reward, the adoption of higher purpose becomes challenging.

In the chapters that follow, we will flesh these ideas out and give you examples of people and organizations that have excelled in the practice of these principles. We will give you specific tools with which you can discover and implement your own higher purpose.

In chapter 2 we discuss the role of the individual in organizational higher purpose.

CHAPTER TWO

Higher Purpose Changes Everything

To understand organizational higher purpose, we need to understand the role of individuals, especially leaders, in the discovery of higher purpose. This chapter is devoted to the role of the individual in organizational higher purpose. For the individual the acquisition of higher purpose in life changes everything.

Leadership and Higher Purpose

When people embrace higher purpose, they begin to transcend convention, access new capacity, and behave in seemingly counterintuitive ways. Conventional economic thinking focuses on *contractual* ways to deal with individual self-interest in organizations and align employee behavior more closely with the behavior the owners of the business want. In this approach, employee self-interest is *taken as a given*, and the goal is to design employment contracts that do the best job of bridging the divide between those who own productive resources and those who manage them to produce economic value.

If we study purpose-driven CEOs, we begin to uncover an alternative worldview. Purpose-driven CEOs do not reject conventional economic thinking. They transform it, and the change is driven by focused imagination rather than conventional fear. Instead of seeing employees as being purely self-interested, purpose-driven CEOs see them as potentially responding to a call for purpose that is larger than themselves, and even larger than the organization itself. This response creates in their employees a desire to contribute to a legacy, to being part of a larger contribution to society that they can be proud of.

As purpose-driven leaders move forward, they build purpose-driven organizations. But this is not easy. The challenge they face is that they confront the paradox we discussed in the previous chapter. How do you pursue organizational higher purpose in light of the demands of your investors to produce tangible economic results that may be jeopardized by pursuing higher purpose? In this chapter we show how the paradox can be confronted. We show how embracing a higher purpose transforms human perspective and how scientific research supports our claims.

People and Purpose

One day when we were talking with undergraduate students at the Center for Positive Organizations at the Ross School of Business at the University of Michigan, the students expressed anxiety about their careers. We told them that when you live a life of higher purpose, a life of meaningful contribution, a transformation occurs. Work is no longer an exercise in dreadful labor, an economic exchange for money. *Work becomes a pleasure because the more you do it, the more you actualize your potential.* You create and discover a more dynamic and virtuous self. You experience more self-respect, and you have more respect for others.

When you love what you do, extrinsic rewards such as wealth and power become less motivational. You begin to orient to intrinsic motivators such as meaning, integrity, love, and learning. You are thus less determined by your culture and more able to shape the culture in which you operate. That is, you become a leader, a person who effectively invites others to make new, good things happen.

When you make this shift, you have more and more opportunities to contribute to others. You spend more time in a self-reinforcing, positive cycle. This does not mean you have no challenges. It does mean that you tend to have the energy to fight through your challenges. When you have a clear purpose and love pursuing it, you become ever more masterful at making contributions that matter. You begin to live for significance rather than success.

A Practical Question

In a session with undergraduates about personal purpose, we were asked a practical question: "How do you find your life purpose?" Bob responded by telling a story.

> One day our daughter, Shauri, called to tell us her boyfriend had just broken off their relationship. She was churning with negative feelings. She announced she was coming home to recover. The next morning, I went to the airport.
>
> She climbed into the car and immediately started talking about her unfortunate situation. She was in a deep emotional hole, and as she agonized, the hole seemed only to get deeper and darker. Finally, I asked her if she was problem solving or purpose finding. The strange question jolted her, and she looked at me quizzically.
>
> I suggested that most people tend to live their lives in a reactive mode. They are always trying to solve their problems. People are sad or happy depending on where they are in the ebb and flow. This is very common. Normal people tend to live in the reactive state.
>
> I suggested an alternative. We can become initiators or creators of our own lives. When we initiate, we tend to eventually create value, and we tend to feel good about ourselves. If we continually clarify our purpose, we live with vision. We are drawn to the future we imagine. We begin to pursue our purpose, and our negative

emotions tend to occur less frequently. We experience victory over the reactive self, and we feel good about who we are. We feel better because we literally begin to have a more valuable self. We are empowered, and we become empowering to others.

Shauri was not buying it. She ignored me and spent another 15 minutes questioning her self-worth. She paused for a breath, and I again asked her if she was problem solving or purpose finding. She ignored my question and continued wondering whether what had happened to her happened because she "was not good enough."

We repeated this pattern four times. The last time I asked, she stopped talking and just looked at me. I could tell a big challenge was coming.

In order to stop my insensitive questions, she asked, "How would I ever use purpose finding in this situation?"

"You can use it in any situation," I replied.

"How do you do it?"

"Whenever I am feeling lost or filled with negative emotions, I get out my life statement and I rewrite it."

Just then we were turning into the driveway. She asked me, "What is a life statement?"

I explained that it is a short document in which you try to capture the essence of who you are and what your purpose is in life.

"You have an actual document that does that?" She seemed truly surprised.

Something had changed. I had her attention. She was expressing genuine curiosity. Here was a chance for meaningful contact and the exploration of profound possibility.

"Let me show you my life statement," I said.

She followed me into my study. I reached into a file, pulled out a sheet of paper, and handed it to her. Shauri read the document carefully and then looked up. She asked, "When you feel bad, you read this, and it makes you feel better?"

"No, when I feel really bad, I rewrite some part of it or add something new. The document is always evolving. When I finish, I feel clearer about who I am. By clarifying what I most value, I become more stable. When I clarify my purpose and my values, I center myself. My negative emotions tend to disappear before I even start to act. Just clarifying who I am and what I want to create seems to energize me. Even the thought of movement becomes uplifting.

"There is another reason for rewriting," I continued. "People think that values are permanent, like cement. Clear values can stabilize us, yet they are not cement. They need to evolve. Each time we face a new situation and reinterpret our values, they change just a little bit. Rewriting a statement like this one allows us to integrate what we have learned and how we have developed into our values. Hence, our values also evolve with us. We co-create each other."

I told Shauri that I have executives in my classes write their life statements, and they find it hard. They begin with very simple life statements.

I suggested that instead of spending the weekend feeling bad about what happened and working through all her reactions to the event, she might instead spend her time writing her own life statement. What happened next is telling.

Shauri finished writing her life statement and headed home. A few days later she sent me a copy of an amazing letter. She has given me permission to share it.

She began it by describing her painful experience and her decision to fly home:

> Dad picked me up from the airport, and on the way home he started to ask me questions about what and how I was feeling about the situation with Matt. At first the focus was just on the pain I was feeling and the self-pity. I wondered what was wrong with me and if I would ever find anyone to love. I was just going over and over the problem.
>
> Dad turned the conversation from solving my problem to finding my purpose. My gut reaction initially was to bring it back to the problem. I wanted to wallow in the pain of the

> problem. I thought I was looking for a solution, but it wasn't
> until I allowed the conversation to really flow into my purpose
> that I found the solution.[4]

Negative emotions pull us into a reactive mode. They drain us of energy and lead us to ruminate on the problem.[5] They cause us to go around in circles. When Shauri at last found her purpose, her entire outlook changed. She began to rise above her day-to-day problems. She shifted from problem solving to purpose finding.

Shauri's letter brought about a surprising turn of events. She shared an email message she had recently sent to her old boyfriend. It turns out that he had contacted her and indicated he missed hearing from her. In response she wrote an unusually open, authentic, and seemingly vulnerable letter.

When her roommates saw the letter, they argued that the message was too honest! They could never imagine opening themselves up to someone who had just rejected them. In coming to this conclusion, they were making conventional assumptions: Dating is a marketplace of self-interested search. It is a transactional process—when someone dumps you, you respond in a way the person deserves.

Previously, Shauri might have agreed. Yet something had changed. She was suddenly less normal, less fearful, less driven by a need for justice. What Shauri wrote to me next is of great consequence.

> The funny thing is I felt a huge sense of peace about it all. It was
> liberating. . . . I was no longer worried about his response or reac-
> tion to me or to what I told him. I chose to act rather than react.
> Because I did, it freed me and empowered me. By giving up control
> in this situation I gained control of the situation. I wasn't worried
> about his response. I had been completely honest with him, and
> strangely it gave me confidence.
>
> My purpose is to purify myself of ego and to serve others. Since
> I began working toward purpose, I have been set free from my

problems, and they are resolving themselves. I feel filled with light and I know that as I continue in my purpose my light will grow brighter and brighter and I will lose myself in it.

Shauri's experience illustrates some important points. First, it is normal to be reactive and to have negative emotions. We are all pulled in this direction. While most of us would claim that we hate the negative emotions we are feeling, we do not behave as if we do. In fact, we often choose to stay in our negative state. We seem to become addicted to the process of wallowing in "the problem." It is natural and, in a strange way, it is comfortable to be in such pain. At such times, this victim role is our path of least resistance, so we willingly take it, perhaps because it is a role we know how to play.

Second, we can control our being state. We do not have to stay in the victim role. We can choose our own response. We do this by leaving the external world, where it can seem to us the problem is located. We go inside ourselves, not to the problem but to our imagined purpose. When we go inside to clarify our purpose, our perception alters dramatically.[6] The original problem does not necessarily go away, but it becomes much less relevant. We outgrow the problem.

Third, changing our being state changes the world. As soon as Shauri started to clarify her purpose, her negative emotions turned positive. She felt more empowered and empowering. To become more empowering is to become a leader, someone who helps others empower themselves.

Why do we believe that Shauri made these three changes? Shortly after her change in outlook, we saw a change in her professional life. She brought initiative and creativity to her job. She was promoted, and her career took a sharp upward turn, a turn she had not previously imagined.

In her new job, she presented herself in a much more peaceful and confident way. The new Shauri was more valuable to her company than was the old Shauri. The new, purpose-driven Shauri was making the company more effective, and they needed her emerging leadership at a higher level.

Personal Payoffs

In sharing the story about Shauri, we are making a lot of claims about the payoffs of finding higher purpose. Scientific research suggests that our claims are generalizable but not comprehensive. There are actually many more payoffs. In his book *Life on Purpose: How Living for What Matters Most Changes Everything,*[7] our colleague Vic Strecher reviews the scientific literature on some of the benefits of having a life purpose.

The research suggests that having an authentic higher purpose will do the following: add years to your life, reduce the risk of heart attack and stroke, cut your risk of Alzheimer's disease, increase sexual enjoyment, help you sleep better at night, reduce the likelihood of depression, increase your chances of staying drug or alcohol free after treatment, activate your natural killer cells and diminish your inflammatory cells, and increase your good cholesterol. It has also been found that higher purpose or prosocial motivation predicts persistence, performance, and productivity.[8]

People with a purpose in life stay more optimistic in the face of adversity. Research shows that optimism is often a self-fulfilling prophecy—your optimism about the future generates a stronger commitment to working to achieve the positive outcomes you are more optimistic about.[9] For example, if you think you are going to live longer, you invest more in going to the gym, which makes you healthier, and you may actually live longer! A person with an authentic higher purpose in many ways functions above the norm or outside convention. The person accesses valuable life assets. The data suggest that we are designed by nature to transcend nature.

Purpose and Leadership

When Shauri embraced purpose, her perspective changed and she found new capacity, and she began to conduct herself more effectively. As the research suggests, she was more optimistic, she was more oriented to commitment and achievement, she behaved in new ways, she performed beyond expectations, and she drew new resources into her life.

She also began to lead other people. As you will see in this book, finding personal purpose often transforms a person, and they begin to lead. This transformation, as we will also see in this book, is true even for CEOs. When they finally discover purpose, their perspective changes, and they seek to create a purpose-driven organization.

Purpose and the Organization

The notion of a purpose-driven organization raises an interesting possibility. Is it possible to create a social system in which there is a culture of excellence? Is it possible to create an organization that regularly exceeds expectations because the personal interest and the collective interests are one? Is it possible to have a workforce that is so optimistic and committed that the organization exceeds financial expectations and holds together when others would begin to splinter?

The answers to all these questions are in the affirmative. In the chapters that follow, we will see numerous case studies that provide examples.

Benefits of Higher Purpose

An organization benefits from having an authentic higher purpose in two main ways. First, an authentic purpose binds people together, forming a "moral glue" and inspiring employees. People are motivated to act in the collective interest of the organization rather than to pursue narrow self-interest. People do not cut corners ethically because they know that doing so is not consistent with the culture of the organization and that their fellow workers will not endorse them in doing so.

In an organization of higher purpose, employees expect one another to do the right thing. Employees work harder, do less to sabotage one another in competitive intraorganizational games, and are more likely to stay with the organization, meaning lower turnover of valued employees. As a result, the economic output of the organization increases. In one organization we worked with, the CEO told us about how higher purpose had changed the culture: "Now when they have a conflict, they just ask what I would say if I were there, and most of the time they know the answer. So I do not have to arbitrate disputes. People sort things out. There is no backstabbing where people come to me to complain about others." The result is a strong focus and energy that flows toward the goal of exceeding customer expectations.

The claim that purpose-driven leaders are able to achieve these outcomes is supported by large-sample research. A survey of 20,000 employees across 25 industries suggests that people in positions of authority who have clarity of purpose and communicate it have great impact on the workforce. Employees of purpose-driven leaders are reportedly 70 percent more satisfied, 56 percent more engaged, and 100 percent more likely to stay with the organization.[10]

Second, an authentic organizational higher purpose helps to clarify the organization's deepest intent to external stakeholders. This clarity reduces conflicts with those stakeholders, including public regulators, competitors, suppliers, and customers. Just think of the scandals involving systematic falsification of emissions data by Volkswagen, Toyota's accidents in North America involving stuck gas pedals in its cars, and the huge fines and negative publicity that many financial institutions were subjected to in the aftermath of the 2007 to 2009 financial crisis.

These incidents were very damaging to these organizations in a tangible economic sense. By contrast, Southwest Airlines, which has a much better reputation than most companies for an organizational higher purpose that attends to both employees and customers, has been able to do things other organizations cannot do.

Higher Purpose and Economic Performance

An organizational higher purpose is *neither charity nor a panacea for doing well*. To do well, the organization needs all the other business capabilities: a core competence, a strategy tied to that core competence, a good product, the ability to execute plans, sound financial management, and operational excellence. Moreover, what we seek is an understanding of the *intersection* of higher purpose and business strategy, not some charitable cause distinct from the company's business. Thus, the organization must stress operational and economic success while it embraces higher purpose. In fact, it is hard to imagine an organization being able to make the short-run sacrifices in pursuit of higher purpose unless it is also financially healthy in the long run.

An organization can embrace an authentic higher purpose, but that purpose has to also make economic sense in the overall business of the organization. A nice illustration of this is provided by an episode of *Shark Tank*, in which a farmer named Johnny Georges, who had invented a tepee that would cover trees that were being watered in the field in order to conserve water used in irrigation, was seeking funding from the sharks to grow the business. The product was called "tree T-PEE," and it was an ingenious yet strikingly simple water and nutrient containment system.

Georges's stated higher purpose was to conserve water in farming and to better serve farmers. The sharks asked him how much it cost to make each unit of the product and how much he was charging for it. They thought he was charging too little—the profit margin was too low. But he kept saying that these were *farmers* he was serving, and he did not want to gouge them with higher prices. Shark after shark turned down the request for funding because of the perceived lack of commercial viability and the seeming impossibility of scaling up the business with such low profit margins. Eventually, one shark, John Paul DeJoria, stepped up and provided funding, insisting, however, that the selling price would have to be raised to a level Georges was comfortable with but higher than what was currently being charged. The business went on to become successful. The day after the episode of *Shark Tank* aired, Georges's inbox was flooded with more than 56,000 emails, and he sold thousands of tree T-PEEs that night. The product is now sold internationally, and Georges has a secured a deal with Home Depot.[11]

This example illustrates the importance of the word *economics* in the statement of corporate higher purpose. Pursuit of higher purpose is not charity. If you're a manufacturer, you don't need to give the product away. Having a profitable business does not conflict with the pursuit of higher purpose.

We now turn to the issue of imagination.

Imagining Organizations of Higher Purpose

Henry Ford said, "If I asked the customer what he wanted he would have said, 'a faster horse.'" A person who has never imagined an automobile cannot ask for one; they can only ask for a better or faster version of what they already comprehend. Because they make conventional assumptions, they can only aspire to incremental changes or small improvements.

This limitation also applies to the subject of this book. Authentic higher purpose, as we saw in chapter 1, transcends conventional assumptions. The notion tends to defy normal understanding, imply accountability, and spur resistance.

Imagining the Unimaginable

It is difficult to imagine a person of authentic higher purpose, and it is difficult to imagine an organization of authentic higher purpose. When Shauri was invited to engage in purpose finding she resisted with vigor. She could not imagine how to create and live from an authentic higher purpose, so she remained in a reactive state. She was behaving conventionally. Shauri's story is that of a young woman, a first-line employee who cannot imagine living in a higher state. It is understandable that she would be trapped in convention. She is not the only one who has trouble imagining a higher state. This book partially flows from a discovery we made when we interviewed CEOs of organizations driven by an authentic higher purpose.

Our surprising finding is that more than half of the CEOs we interviewed were just like Shauri, the first-line employee. When they first became CEOs, they had heard of purpose but did not understand its power, and thus did not want to invest in finding it. As with most people, they became purpose driven through crisis and deep learning.

One of these CEOs is Alberto Weisser, the retired CEO of Bunge, a global food company.[12] In Alberto's 11 years as CEO, the company grew by a factor of 10. Between the time it went public in 2001 and the time of his retirement in 2013, the stock price had increased fivefold.

Alberto's story appears to be a saga of uninterrupted success. It was not. In fact, his first year as CEO was one of the most difficult of his life. He was failing because of something he could not imagine.

Alberto's career was in finance. He was CFO before being promoted to CEO. He was a master of the conventional economic perspective, and that had carried him up the corporate ladder. Given his training, he believed that an organization is a hierarchy of authority. The person at the top gives orders, and the people below follow them. If there is resistance, the CEO has to be tough.

Alberto was tough, yet he was failing. As he applied his conventional ideas of hierarchy, authority, and toughness, the organization failed to perform. This failure challenged his theory of leadership, and it eventually transformed his way of seeing the world. Alberto eventually became a purpose-driven leader who could imbue an organization with authentic higher purpose, but getting there was not easy.

Looking back, Alberto says, "I was overwhelmed and I was scared." We tend to think of CEOs as people in positions of power who are immune to being scared. Yet the role of a CEO is to lead change. Leading change means inviting people into unique challenges and deep learning. It is a fearful thing when facts begin to tell you that you do not know how to perform your primary professional function.

That fear is greatly increased as you begin to realize that the beliefs that brought you to your current professional position are actually the source of your failure. Suddenly you are living in a terrible paradox, and the only way out is deep or transformative learning, which requires mindful reflection and personal discipline. It means that you come to see something you cannot imagine.

Alberto continued, saying, "I was simpleminded." *Simpleminded* does not mean stupid. One does not climb to the top of a corporation by being stupid. In fact, Alberto was quite brilliant. When it came to finance, he had a complex mental map that allowed him to do things others could not do. Alberto could take the most difficult financial challenges and come up with brilliant solutions.

In this context, *simpleminded* means being unsophisticated about something. It means being unaware and failing to see parts of reality that are important. It means not seeing the dynamic whole. Alberto was "simpleminded" because he had a conventional, mind-set that limited the range of his influence. His mind-set, which was heavily influenced by traditional economics, had led him to success as a young professional and now blinded him to what he needed to know and do in order to be successful as a CEO.

The Conventional Economic Mind-Set

The lesson here is that economics is a highly sophisticated field of thought. It emerges from the rigorous examination of social and financial reality. The conventional economic mind-set is the foundation of business education, and it gives rise to the language and practice of business. It is based on many explicit and implicit assumptions, such as the following:

The Conventional Mind-Set

➤ The typical organization is a structured hierarchy.

➤ People are risk averse and self-interested (i.e., they maximize their own expected utility).

➤ People work for monetary rewards and minimize personal costs because doing so increases expected utility.

➤ People compete for resources because greater resources yield higher compensation, organizational power, and other perks (all of which increase expected utility).

➤ People hold on to the status quo because they are risk averse and change increases uncertainty, which decreases the expected utility.

➤ People underperform because they perceive themselves as toiling for others (i.e., they are agents of others rather than owners or principals).

How can the assumptions in this list impede our success as leaders?

Conventional means "usual," "normal," "established," "standard." If we examine normal experience, we find the patterns listed above. Self-interested people seeking survival in a hierarchy tend toward political compromise and compliance with expectations. The culture drives behavior. As managers engage in problem solving, they become extensions of the culture. They become instruments seeking to restore equilibrium and control. The thought process that underlies the problem solving begins with the transactional assumptions listed above and ensures that the status quo survives.

Academic disciplines teach rigorous analysis based on these transactional assumptions. A person who learns economics and other related fields gains knowledge that first increases the ability to create value and that then, paradoxically, begins to decrease the capacity to create value. The discipline first turns the novice into an expert analyst or problem solver, a person like Alberto who creates value and moves up within the expectations of the culture.

As the person moves toward the top, they need a new, more complex, and even paradoxical mind-set. A leader must be able to simultaneously maintain and destroy culture. They must maintain order through conventional thought and hierarchical practices while simultaneously inspiring people to move into uncertainty, learn, and innovate.

This ability to maintain order and inspire change cannot be done by fiat. The leader must have vision, purpose, and inspiration. They must integrate images of a desired future with the existing images of a constrained present. They must have awareness of interpersonal relations and the ability to influence without authority.

Experimental research shows that when people are in the conventional economic mind-set, they have less empathy.[13] The people affected by the analytical decisions also have less awareness. Leaders in the conventional mind-set construct people as objects to be acted upon. Robert Chapman, CEO of Barry-Wehmiller, is a purpose-driven leader who rejects this mind-set. He told us: "I learned nothing about leadership from business school. Everything I learned about leadership came from parenting."

The conventional mind-set precludes the notion of authentic higher purpose. It negates the pursuit of prosocial behavior. It is based on the above assumptions of self-interest, scarcity, and competition, and it tends to produce what is assumed.

Seeing Conventional Reality

Why does the conventional mind-set preclude the adoption of an authentic higher purpose? One possibility is that there is a sorting effect as people move up the hierarchy. Those who, like Alberto, are task focused and achievement oriented tend to be more likely to succeed early in their careers, especially in achieving readily observable tangible outcomes. This success helps them get promoted by people who themselves seek to be promoted and care primarily about measurable economic outcomes.

If the organization's culture values individual achievement, numbers tend to be all that matter, and people who produce the numbers get promoted and rewarded. That is, incentives are "high powered."[14] Employees seek to emulate those people, further reinforcing the numbers-driven culture. Yet this narrow and conventional focus destroys relationships, and the numbers eventually fall.

Unfortunately, this paradoxical dynamic is invisible to the people who produce it. The people who are promoted generally attribute all their successes to their own abilities. Hence, they rise to the top with little appreciation of the "hidden factors" that contributed to their success, namely the culture of the organization and the contributions of others. Psychologists call this "attribution bias."

When such people become CEOs, they often do not appreciate the role of culture or higher purpose. They are unable, for example, to transform a culture of self-interest into a culture of collaboration. Like Alberto, they cannot move the organization because they cannot produce an authentic higher purpose or the moral power necessary to change the existing culture.

When these people encounter a cultural problem, they usually respond by producing more analysis of the technical and financial systems, which are central to the conventional mind-set. They may eventually realize the value of a more positive culture and the importance of collaboration, but they do not know how to change the culture. Their "rationality" in dealing with the problem exacerbates the already widening mismatch with social reality. A vicious cycle emerges and sucks the organization into a whirlpool of increasing tension, conflict, and decay. The organization, which has become divided and distrustful, underperforms its potential. The conventional economic mind-set, encouraged by the authority figure who once created value, is then destroying value. The authority figure cannot understand why.

We do not mean to denigrate rigorous thought and economic

analysis or ask people to abandon these. To the contrary, we continue to advocate the rigorous tools of economics and the related disciplines. But what we are calling for is for people to augment traditional economic analysis and access a more complete and dynamic form of understanding and influence. To obtain that understanding, you must transcend the conventional mind-set and come to imagine what the conventional mind-set precludes.[15]

From Knowing to Learning

At the end of our interview with Alberto, he reflected on his learning journey. He said that of all the assumptions in the conventional economic mind-set, there was one that was more problematic than any other. His conventional mind-set told him that he had to be "the expert." As the leader, he needed to have all the answers. This assumption, more than any other, accounted for his initial failure. He said, "If you are an imperial CEO, or if you think too much of yourself, then it doesn't work."

The need to be an expert, someone who is in control and does not fail, is a natural consequence of the conventional mind-set. It is not a problem limited to CEOs. It permeates the culture and applies to everyone.

From the time we learn to talk, we internalize the conventional mind-set. We learn from our parents that life is hierarchical—such as when we're told "Because I told you so." We learn that it is better to be on top of a hierarchy than on the bottom: "I am the boss." We learn that people are self-interested, and outcomes must be negotiated as in the parental edict: "If you want dessert, you have to eat what is on your plate." We learn that resources are scarce: "No, you cannot have it. Money does not grow on trees." We learn that conflict is natural: "Share it with your brother, or I will take it away."

Then we get educated. If we go to business school, for example, during the first hour of the first day we encounter the culture of knowing. We learn immediately that you always have to be smart, to know the right answer to every question. We spend two years continually posturing, pretending that we know and living with the fear of being exposed. Nothing is dreaded more than the teacher who cold-calls (requests information from students regardless of whether they have their hands in the air). Such a teacher is a constant threat to the ego.

When we leave business school and enter organizations, we often encounter the same culture of knowing. We hear people speak admiringly of others: "He is really smart!" or "Ask her. She knows everything!" The message is clear: if someone has a position of authority or is on a fast track for promotions, they should know everything regarding their stewardship. This assumption leads to elaborate rituals that emerge to protect powerful people. We should never be in a situation that reveals our ignorance.

The problem with a culture of knowing is that it prevents the emergence of a culture of learning. When people like Alberto believe they must be the expert, information flows down in the organization. It flows up in highly filtered ways.

From Exclusive to Inclusive

The conventional mind-set is ego driven. It assumes that one person acts on the whole and controls it. This assumption ignores the fact that influence flows in every direction. Everyone is shaping everyone else, including the person at the top. The organization is a function of many conversations occurring simultaneously, and the learning is reciprocal. This process is not mechanistic but rather is complex and adaptive. The quality of these conversations has much to do with how the organization performs.

The conventional mind-set sees the manager as an extension of the culture. Most recognize that the culture exists, but they accept the culture as bigger than they are. They cannot imagine the capacity to *create* culture. They lack what we call "cultural self-efficacy," the confidence that they can create culture. When they lack cultural self-efficacy, culture change is seen as the job of someone at the top.

Leadership requires you to adopt the positive mind-set and have the ability to imagine and create what may be outside the current culture. A leader with a positive mind-set makes assumptions such as the following:

The Positive Mind-Set

➢ An organization is a dynamic social system.

➢ People can become selfless contributors.

➢ People will sacrifice for a higher purpose.

➢ People can invest their discretionary energy.

➢ People can collaborate and co-create.

➢ People can become inspired and fully engaged.

➢ People can grow and flourish at work.

➢ People can exceed expectations.

The Inclusive Mind-Set

Alberto made another point that was seemingly insignificant and easy to ignore but turned out to be quite important. Alberto told us that he does not always speak to others the way he was speaking to us. Many of the people he deals with are still embedded in the conventional mind-set. They are, in his terms, "simpleminded." They remain as blind as he was.

He said he has to take that into account and adjust how he communicates. He can do it because he was once where they are now. Alberto can still speak the managerial language of control and constraint, but he can also provide the kind of direction that empowers people and enables the organization to grow.

Because of his deep learning, Alberto can see multiple realities and speak both the conventional language of management and the unconventional language of leadership. He can meet people where they are and work with them in a way that changes the culture. Alberto is operating from a more positive, complex, and dynamic mind-set. He accepts the constraints of convention and the realities of possibility. He is an intelligent optimist. He is living from the positive mind-set and he is able to make more complex assumptions such as the following:

The Inclusive Mind-Set

➤ While an organization is a structured hierarchy, it is also a dynamic social system.

➤ While people are self-interested, they can also be motivated by an organizational higher purpose to subordinate their narrow self-interests for the greater whole.

➤ While people work for money, they will also sacrifice for a higher purpose and a sense of meaning.

➤ While people seek to minimize costs and compete for resources, they can also collaborate for the good of the organization and the common higher purpose.

➤ While people become alienated, they also can become inspired by the organizational higher purpose and become fully engaged.

➤ While people hold to the status quo, they can also engage with challenges and initiate change.

➤ While people can stagnate and underperform, they can also overcome agency problems and grow and flourish at work.

The conventional mind-set is exclusive and based on either/or thinking. The more positive, inclusive mind-set is based not on either/or thinking but on both/and thinking. Taking the inclusive mind-set does not exclude the conventional mind-set. When we acquire the inclusive mind-set, we simply become more cognitively complex. We lose nothing. Like Shauri and like Alberto, we continue to recognize convention, but we can also imagine and do things outside of convention. We can appreciate the past while we conceptualize the future.

An Inclusive Economics

We have seen that when you find an authentic higher purpose, you acquire new feelings and thoughts. When you articulate and embrace a higher purpose, you enter a new life path. You discard the assumptions that people maximize expected utility only through their explicit compensation and promotion rewards, that they are always competing for limited resources, and that they want to hold on to the status quo.

When people pursue an authentic higher purpose, they gain utility that is directly generated by that pursuit, so what they view as being in their own self-interest moves closer to the prosocial higher purpose of the organization. They see intrinsic personal rewards that go beyond the explicit compensation and promotion rewards and that are provided by the pursuit of the higher purpose. They derive less personal utility from denying resources to others in the organization who are also pursuing the same higher purpose. They are less likely to compete and more likely to collaborate.

As people pursue authentic purpose, they experience deep learning. In the process, they create and discover a new, more dynamic, and empowered self, and they begin to pursue what cannot be imagined or pursued from a conventional perspective. They see the possibility of organizational excellence, networks of people linked to a higher purpose, demonstrations of resilience, engagement in learning, and collaboration as they create patterns of higher performance. In this process, they transcend the conventional mind-set. They take on a more positive, complex, and dynamic mind-set. Contrast this with the standard economic paradigm of organizational behavior, which we turn to in the next chapter.

CHAPTER FOUR

Transforming Self-Interest

Imagine a hot day, with the sun blazing brightly. A sharecropper is toiling in the field, working hard. He would love to take a breather and relax under the cool shade of a nearby tree, but he will be paid at the end of the day based on how much he harvests. He has a family to feed, and the more he harvests, the more wages he makes. He decides he can rest when he gets home in the evening. Now it is time to work hard and harvest as much as he can before dusk. This is, of course, precisely how the landowner would like the share-cropper to reason—work harder and get paid more; goof off and get paid less.

This story illustrates the workhorse model in economics that describes the relationship between employers and employees. It is called the principal–agent model,[16] and multiple Nobel Prizes in economics have been awarded for contributions to the development of it. It offers powerful insights.

When a person is employed by an organization, the organization recognizes that the person is effort averse, that is, they prefer less work to more. All else being equal, the person will shirk when it comes to working for the organization. Because the organization wants the individual to work hard, it must make it in the best inter-est of that individual to do so. In other words, in the context of the assumptions we discussed in chapter 3, the individual maximizes expected utility (defined over their wealth or consumption) and minimizes the cost in terms of personal effort. Moreover, the organization is a hierarchy—the sharecropper has a boss, the landowner.

To get the individual to work hard, the organization typically uses two practices: input monitoring and output incentives.[17] It practices input monitoring by watching over the employees to see how hard they are working. Imagine the landowner patrolling the fields to see how hard the sharecropper is working. Analytical Alberto exercised this type of control over the organization. It also practices output incentives by giving the employee a compensation reward that increases as the observed output increases. Output incentives make it unnecessary for managers to watch the employee all the time to see how hard they are working.

The principal–agent model is a workhorse model of employer-employee relationships in economics because it describes behavior well, it is elegant and tractable, and it provides valuable insights about how to design not only labor contracts but also a host of financial contracts. For example, it helps us understand why executives should be given bonuses and stock options, and why vesting schedules are often structured the way they are. It explains why insurance contracts have deductibles.

An essential element of the model is moral hazard. *Moral* means "ethical," "good," "right," "honorable," or "principled." *Hazard* means "danger," "exposure," "vulnerability," "threat," "risk," or "peril." Thus, *moral hazard* means that moral behavior is imperiled. A moral hazard arises when an individual chooses self-interest over the collective interest and acts in a manner that violates the *spirit* of the contractual relationship, although not necessarily the legal aspects of the contract itself.

This selfishness is powerful and contagious. For example when a boss chooses self-interest over the collective interest, the direct report reciprocates. The direct report pursues self-interest too, even if doing so sacrifices the common good. Over time, pursuing self-interest becomes the culture of the organization, its social contract.

Unity is lost, and the social network is frayed. When this fraying occurs, the individual and the system become less productive. If the choice of self-interest spreads, the organization loses unified effort, and it becomes a collection of individuals all seeking their self-interest. Alberto came to realize the consequences of this loss of unity after his initial experience as a CEO.

People who have a conventional mind-set pursue self-interest. Absent output-based rewards or input monitoring, the sharecropper goofs off. Absent deductibles, the insured will "overuse" insurance. The classic illustration of overuse is a person driving their car into a lake and then reporting it as stolen in order to collect the insurance money because the car was worth less than the insured value. Overuse is also observed in health insurance: absent copay provisions, people tend to overuse medical services.

The principal–agent model says that the party in the contracting relationship that suffers due to the moral hazard—the employer or the insurance company—is "smart" enough to recognize the moral hazard and design input monitoring and output-based contracts to attenuate its effects. This attenuation leads to what is called a "non-cooperative Nash equilibrium" in which the employer anticipates the employee's strategic behavior and then designs a contract to attenuate the effects of that behavior, and the employee behaves in exactly the manner the employer anticipated.

John Nash (the mathematician depicted in *A Beautiful Mind*) came up with this concept to describe the kind of equilibrium that relationships settle into when each party acts in their own self-interest and the other party recognizes this and therefore acts the same way. In the sharecropper example, if the landowner mistakenly pays the sharecropper a fixed wage and then is too busy one day to monitor his activity, the sharecropper will indeed goof off, validating the landowner's expectation of his behavior.

The sharecropper's view is that a landowner interested in maximizing crop output would either pay him more for producing more or watch over him more closely, so if the landowner is doing neither, then why not goof off? The sharecropper rationally expects the landowner to view the sharecropper as being self-interested, and the landowner rationally expects the sharecropper to view the landowner as being self-interested; caring only about profit (and not the sharecropper's welfare). An equilibrium is reached when each party's expectation about how the other will behave is indeed the way each party behaves.

Why the Principal–Agent Model Was Created: It's Better Than the Alternatives

Before we explain how the principal–agent model should be modified to incorporate higher purpose, we note that it was developed to fill a need in economics to have a framework within which we could understand how to deal contractually with self-interested behavior. That is, the model highlighted a prevalent problem and showed that contracts could be designed to deal with it. The first and most profound insight of the principal–agent model is that incentives matter because people respond to incentives in their contracts. The second major insight is that people are both effort averse and risk averse. So they will work hard only if by doing so they perceive they will be better off, and they dislike uncertainty in the compensation they receive for working hard.

First, the point that individuals respond to contractual incentives is empirically valid. For example, the Health and Medicine Division (formerly the Institute for Medicine) estimates that unnecessary medical services, excessive administrative costs, and fraud account for about $300 billion a year in health-care spending in the United States, which was about 30 percent of the total spending on health care in 2009.[18] Some observers have suggested that much of this is due to perverse economic incentives generated by contractual features embedded in the current system.[19] One of these contractual features is fee-for-service payments to doctors that encourage potentially unnecessary services. Another is copayments by patients that may be too small to discourage them from asking for unnecessary and expensive medical services.

For example, a doctor told us he was working the night shift in the emergency room of a hospital. A woman came in late at night with a cut she had suffered on a finger. This was something she could have taken care of herself and then gone to her doctor in the morning to get a checkup to see if anything else was needed. Instead, relying on laws that require her to be treated without question, she came to the emergency room. When the doctor was done treating her, he asked, "Why did you come to the emergency room for this? You could have just gone to your doctor in the morning. This was not an emergency." She responded, "Doctor, that would have meant taking two hours away from work, for which I would lose pay, and then I would be seen by a nurse practitioner only. By coming to the emergency room, I don't lose time away from work and a real doctor treats me."

This is rational behavior on her part, but such behavior by many people leads to huge negative externalities for the whole system, driving up health-care costs and possibly denying someone really in need of emergency medical services timely access to a doctor. This is the power of incentives at work. When we build bad incentive systems, we get bad behavior. That is exactly what the principal–agent model predicts.

Second, perhaps the strongest evidence in support of aversion to effort and risk is that people buy insurance of all sorts. If you are not risk averse, you do not need insurance. Moreover, the insight that individuals are effort averse and will not work hard unless incentivized by their wage contract to do so is also empirically supported. One study used data from a windshield fitting company to estimate the change in performance that occurred when the firm introduced piece-rate compensation. Productivity rose by about 35 percent.[20] Another study used data on tree planters in British Columbia, where in some instances piece rates were used, and in others fixed wages were used. The incentive effects of piece rates led to behavioral changes that accounted for between 6 percent and 35 percent increases in productivity.[21] Yet another study of British jockeys showed that the use of bonuses attached to victories improved performance.[22]

Numerous other studies argue against incentives. They find that incentives may be counterproductive and may cause employees to focus on the wrong things—driving only measured performance at the expense of important output variables that are difficult to measure and not included in computing bonuses. However, economists George Baker, Michael Jensen, and Kevin Murphy suggest that this is not an indictment of incentives but rather a statement that perhaps incentives work too well.[23] That is, you need to design incentives in compensation contracts to incentivize the behavior you want—behavior that affects both easy-to-measure outputs as well as outputs that are hard to measure—recognizing that the incentives will have powerful effects on behavior.

We do not seek to negate these insights but to take them as a given and build on them. We will show that an important role of higher purpose is to change incentives and influence employee behavior. Moreover, higher purpose may also reduce the uncertainty that employees perceive.

Inefficiencies Due to Contracting Frictions in the Principal–Agent Framework

While an accurate descriptor of behavior on average, the Nash equilibrium in the principal–agent model also involves waste and inefficiency. For example, the output-based contract typically imposes too much risk on the risk-averse employee, even risk that is beyond their control. Think again of the sharecropper. The sharecropper may work really hard, but the weather may turn out to be too hot and dry for a good crop. Output will be low, and the person will make a low wage despite their hard work. They are exposed to the risk of bad weather.

Knowing this, the sharecropper will be unwilling to accept a contract where his wage depends only on output and will need to be paid some amount of fixed wage. Recall the assumption that employees prefer the status quo because it reduces uncertainty. Of course, the bigger the component of his wage that is fixed, the less hard he will work, making the relationship less efficient. A catch-22, indeed!

Moreover, because the employee is effort averse, he tends to minimize effort. That is, he works less hard than he would if he were an employee-owner. He works less hard because when he is an employee-owner, he gets to keep all of the profit from his hard work, whereas when he works for someone else, he has to do the work but share the profit. When organizations expect employees to be narrowly self-interested, employees behave in a way that validates that assumption, and a culture emerges that gives rise to a Nash equilibrium.[24] The conventional culture constrains the emergence of excellence.

This culture of self-interest is the general rule highlighted by the principal–agent model. For example, consider the widely accepted idea that incentives to innovate are typically far stronger for independent entrepreneurs than for the employees of companies. This is an important reason why companies often outsource innovation when speed of innovation is important.

When a company wants to innovate for economic gain, it assumes its self-interested employees will come up with innovations only if they are motivated by the rewards associated with coming up with those breakthroughs, so it will put in place compensation rewards for new ideas. Employees will believe that the only purpose of the innovation is economic gain for the company, so they will work only as hard as the compensation rewards induce them to.

Both the firm and the employees are correct, therefore, in their beliefs about each other. The employees will then compare their personal profit (compensation reward) from innovation within the firm with the personal cost of working hard for it. Because the company will give the employee only a fraction of the profit from the innovation, the reward for the employee is never as great as it would be if the employee were an independent innovator who could keep all of the profit from the innovation for himself. Thus, an independent entrepreneur (who is both a principal and an agent) will always work harder to innovate than an employee (who is only an agent) will.

This sort of equilibrium behavior is costly to the firm, something the principal–agent model recognizes but views as an inevitable consequence of individual self-interest and rational behavior. In some instances, this creates organizational crises that traumatize people.

A Puzzle

A friend of ours, a woman who works on the first line of a large organization, told us of a downsizing that she had experienced. One day the employees were called into a large room. Some people's names were read. These people were asked to walk with security officers to clear their desks and proceed to their cars. They were fired.

As our friend told the story, she began to shake. A year after the event, she was still working for the firm but was still in trauma. She said she has been looking for a new job since that day. She and her peers were, in essence, just going through the motions.

What happened here? The organization's executives, facing a hard problem, did the best they could. They solved their hard problem by using conventional assumptions and executed a conventional solution. In the process they demonstrated a conventional view of work and leadership. Their actions turned the culture more negative. The employees subsequently put in minimum effort and expected similar behavior of one another.

In engaging in a conventional downsizing, the managers destroyed commitment, and they destroyed financial value. Since no one could imagine differently, no one was held accountable for this great destruction of value. They did what they had to do, and in doing so, they failed to take advantage of a great opportunity to create value because they could not imagine the opportunity.

This kind of action not only affects the employees; it also affects the people who execute the strategy. Recently, we spoke with a woman who is a senior HR executive in a Fortune 100 company. She told of a major financial crisis. The company had to downsize, and she led a firing process similar to the one just described. We were surprised to see that as she told the story, she began to shake. Even years after the event and though she was the boss and not the victim, she was traumatized.

For organizations that follow the principal–agent model, these sorts of episodes are predictable. Is there any way out of it? What is a leader to do?

Here is what one purpose-driven leader did. His name is Ricardo Levy. For decades he has been a successful entrepreneur. Today he is retired and he teaches entrepreneurship at Stanford University. Ricardo's company once experienced a financial recession, and he needed to downsize 20 percent of his workforce. He held a meeting to make the announcement. At the conclusion of the meeting, everyone, including the people that were about to be fired, stood up and gave him a standing ovation.

Here is a puzzle: what did Ricardo do?

We have posed this puzzle to many groups of executives, and they look at us in disbelief. We tell them they have three minutes to figure out what Ricardo did. The amazing thing is, in three minutes they move from an inability to imagine such a thing to the correct answer. Their ability to do that suggests that inside all of us is an alternative perspective, a positive mind-set that we often do not access. Stop and think: What is your answer? What did Ricardo do?

An Unconventional Explanation

Ricardo told us that he never kept his people in the dark. He was always transparent and told them the condition of the company. The people also believed him to be fully sincere and genuine. He said,

> I do not use the word *honest* here. I use the word *genuine*. The people can feel it. I guess you could use the word *love*. I loved them, and I loved what I was doing. They absolutely knew I would never take such a step unless there was no other alternative. They knew it was essential for survival, and they knew I was fully aware of the pain I was inflicting. My employees knew from my past actions that I was going to take care, as best as I could, of every one of them. That day I was present with everybody. A leader is not a mechanic. You have to be totally in the moment with your whole being. When you become a leader, you are promising to care for your people and the organization.

Ricardo often uses the word *authentic*. He told us that with authentic leadership you can take your people to an elevated condition. You can leave the transactional world of self-interest. You can provide purpose and vision, and you can connect the people to the highest good. They begin to sacrifice for the authentic purpose, and a sacred space emerges. In that space, you find a community of purpose, trust, transparency. People can tell the truth. People listen. Conflict turns to collaboration and collaboration turns to high performance, and the people live in a valued community of shared identity.

Ricardo violated an assumption of the principal–agent model. He reacted not from self-interest but from care for the common good. If the employees had viewed Ricardo as self-interested, they would have thought that he was downsizing not because it was the only option left but because doing it would increase profits and fatten Ricardo's wallet. They would not have given him a standing ovation when he announced the downsizing. But, more subtly, Ricardo would have anticipated that that is how they would view him and he would have dealt with them accordingly before the downsizing, essentially validating their beliefs, like in the principal–agent model. That would have defined the social contract of the organization. The only way to break out of this self-enforcing system of beliefs is for Ricardo to behave differently before the crisis. He did so by changing his own behavior, changing his own beliefs about his employees, and creating a different relationship with them.

The Covenant of Leadership

Recently, Ricardo faced a new leadership crisis, one that pitted valued relationships against organizational performance. He was deeply torn but forced to decide. He called us and talked through what happened. He said he had had to fearfully step into the unknown—and stay there until he knew what to do. Entering that crucible of transformation, he felt extreme anxiety. As he wrestled with his paradoxical tensions, he could feel a change take place. Suddenly, he knew what to do.

In the transformational moment he gained understanding—complexity reduced to simplicity. His crucible became what he called "a chalice, filled with life-giving refreshment." In describing the transformative moment on the phone, he began to slow as he struggled to express all that had transpired. He was, in real time, learning from his own observations.

In the transformational moment he seemed to be leaving the analytical realm. He was viewing the whole context. His fear turned to confidence, hope, and love. In that moment he also found a new voice: he could suddenly speak both logically and with genuine feeling.

He slowed again as he made sense of what had happened in real time. He mentioned the word *covenant* and paused. Then he said, "When you find the leader within, you discover that you have a covenant. The people expect the leader to see the way, and the leader is promising to do their best to find the way. In uncertainty, this means entering the cauldron and suffering the process of deep learning. The commitment to learning is an act of carrying the people in love."

The Covenant and Community

We were mesmerized by Ricardo's concept of covenant and explored it with him at length. We could see that Ricardo was also trying to fully understand and articulate it. A few days later, he sent us an excited email message with a link to a speech given by Rabbi Lord Jonathan Sacks, which helped Ricardo understand. (The speech was given at the American Enterprise Institute annual dinner in 2017 and can be seen at https://www.youtube.com/watch?v=i347EuoPQJU.)

In the speech, the rabbi, who is also a member of the British House of Lords, gave an extraordinary account of the current American enterprise, its history, and its necessary direction. The words of this "outsider," a British baron and Jewish rabbi, brought a standing ovation from a deeply appreciative American audience. What could he have possibly told Americans about America that would lead to such appreciation?

Rabbi Sacks began by describing the existing politics of anger, disintegration, and conflict that are manifest in America and across the Western world. He then turned to biblical history. He said that democratic capitalism takes root from the Judeo-Christian tradition. Of course, similar notions are also enshrined in other faiths, but they may have had different influences on the governance of the state.

He then turned to the political theory contained in the Hebrew Bible and discussed the founding of the earthly kingdom of Israel. The people told the prophet Samuel they wanted to be like other nations and have a king. God told Samuel that in establishing a king they would be rejecting God. Eventually, they established the kingdom.

In establishing a state, the Israelites were creating a social contract, in essence, the same social contract later articulated by Thomas Hobbes. The people gave up certain rights in exchange for benefits flowing from a centralized authority. In a social contract, each actor seeks self-interest; in commerce, the social contract produces a market; and in politics, the social contract produces a state.

Yet centuries before the Israelites established their state, they established a covenant. A covenant occurs when two or more people come together with respect and trust, and make mutual promises to help one another do what no one can do alone. In this establishment of purpose and action, they shift from "me" to "us." A collective identity emerged. Rabbi Sacks said the idea is well captured in the sacred American phrase "We the people."

A market exists to create and distribute wealth, and a state exists to create and distribute power. A covenant is not about the acquisition of wealth or power. It is about belonging and collective responsibility. While a social contract creates a state, it does not create an integrated system. A covenant brings forth a united society. Because Israel had a covenant society before it had a contractual state, it had a strong collective identity or culture. The collective identity could be maintained even in times of severe challenge.

The notion of a covenant reflects the inclusive mind-set. Covenant and contract can exist in a mutually enhancing relationship. The United States is the only country, other than ancient Israel, that has the dual foundation of covenant and contract. In America, the covenant was established in the Declaration of Independence, and the contract was established in the Constitution. This dual foundation happened because the founding fathers understood that freedom requires both a state (based on contracts) and a society (based on a covenant).

Rabbi Sacks said that today in America and in Europe the social contract remains, but the covenant is in decay. Collective identity is devolving to smaller and smaller groups of self-interest. The lack of a shared moral code does not allow people of different perspectives to "reason together." The ability to listen to a person of a different perspective is crucial to the whole.

The state cannot solve all problems, and those who believe the state can solve all the problems are prone to magical thinking. The far right dreams of "a golden past that never was," and the far left yearns for "a utopian future that never will be." As conflict arises, it gives birth to populism and the hunger for a strong leader who will solve all problems. This hunger leads to a tyranny where the right or left dominates and freedom of expression begins to vanish. Anger replaces reason.

Rabbi Sacks said that the notion of covenant may be difficult to entertain in any country other than the United States because of its history: "We hold these truths to be self-evident that all men are created equal and endowed by their creator with certain inalienable rights." He said that the good news in this time of conflict is that a covenant is renewable. Nations can renew and rebuild community. In a community you have real friends, people you can depend on, people who will care for you when you are in need.

The Possibility of a New Economics

Ricardo and Rabbi Sacks help us understand the covenant of leadership and the emergence of high-performing organizations. The covenant of leadership is a sacred agreement you make with your best self, your dynamic self, your growing self. It gives you the ability to pursue an authentic higher purpose. It gives you the ability to imagine the organization as having a social contract and a social covenant. It gives you the ability to recognize the necessity to continually renew both.

When Shauri discovered her own authentic higher purpose, she made a covenant with herself to become her best self. When Alberto discovered as CEO the difference between his social contract to the organization and his covenant as a leader, it changed him and his ability to lead the organization.

When you establish a covenant that guides the organization, you create an exception to the rule that is the principal–agent model. The covenant inspires employees to transcend the conventional mentality of financial exchange and become intrinsically motivated. It allows them to find a higher purpose in the work, and it alters how they behave. If farmers are harvesting crops only to make money for themselves, they are in an economic exchange. If they believe that in addition to generating profit, the people of their country survive because of their effort, then they may become intrinsically motivated.

Similarly, employees will work harder if they believe that, in addition to producing profit for the firm, the innovation they are seeking will also benefit society. An employee who works hard to come up with a better electric car views that as a contribution to combating climate change. An employee who works hard to develop drugs to cure cancer views that as a way to help prolong people's lives.

Researchers have shown that employees work harder when they view their organization as authentically working for the good of society.[25] The embrace of a *higher purpose* can motivate employees to voluntarily work harder for the common good because individuals also care about things besides explicit compensation rewards—things such as society, integrity, honesty, social identity and reputation, corporate social responsibility, moral behavior, and intrinsic motivation.[26] We build on this idea in chapter 5 in developing an economic theory of higher purpose.

CHAPTER FIVE

Reframing Economics

By "organizational higher purpose," we mean a prosocial goal that transcends the usual pursuit of business goals but intersects with those goals. That is, decisions are made that are in line with prosocial goals as well as the business goals.

John Sculley quotes Steve Jobs about higher purpose: "Great companies must have a noble cause. Then it's the leader's job to transform that noble cause into such an inspiring vision that it will attract the most talented people in the world to want to join it."[27]

We are not interested in examining the consequences of corporate social responsibility or charitable giving. The pursuit of a higher purpose is not a goal—like charitable giving—that is distinct from generating traditional outcomes like profits and shareholder value.[28] Rather, we examine the pursuit of higher purpose that is integrated with the pursuit of business and organizational goals, as in the case of a biotech company working to find a cure for cancer, or the Walt Disney Company creating Disneyland as "a place for people to find happiness and knowledge."[29]

Richard Leider defines higher purpose for individuals this way: "Purpose is the deepest dimension within us—our central core or existence—where we have a profound sense of who we are, where we came from and where we're going. Purpose is the quality we choose to shape our lives around. Purpose is a source of energy and direction."[30]

Leider's observation leads us to ask, How does the adoption of an authentic higher purpose enable an organization to connect to the purpose of its employees? How can the fundamental self-interest assumption of the principal–agent model be modified to produce expanding effort inputs and relaxing budget constraints in a way that leads to superior performance? In answering these questions, in this chapter we will formulate an economic theory of higher purpose, something that Kenneth Boulding called for 50 years ago in his presidential address to the American Economic Association.[31]

Unconventional People

While many people behave in accordance with the predictions of the principal–agent model and do not organize themselves and others to a higher purpose, some, like Ricardo Levy, do, and they acquire a unique kind of influence. The conventional mind-set tells us that people are self-interested. As we saw in previous chapters, our normal experience tends to confirm this. When we encounter a person of higher purpose, someone like Rabbi Sacks, the experience captures our attention. For example, here is an entry that Bob wrote in his personal journal.

> A Woman of Higher Purpose: My daughter-in-law Lisa and my granddaughter Keely went to a mall. In the early evening we received a shocking text: "There are shooters in the mall, pray for us."
>
> This message led to several tense hours. Eventually, Lisa and Keely were able to safely exit.
>
> At dinner the next day, I asked them to tell us the entire story. Lisa shared the account of she and Keely and about 80 other panicked people locking themselves in a back room of a department store. The people pushed a table against the door and spent their time trying to understand what was going on and what to do if the shooters came to the room.

As Lisa told the story, I felt upset, not with just the specifics but with the evil that seems to be growing in the world. Then Lisa added a side note.

Lisa said that as the people in the room made sense of what was happening and considered what to do, a person of her age engaged her. This other woman said, "If they get in the room and start shooting, you stand in front of your daughter and I will stand in front of you."

Lisa was shocked and asked why. The woman said, "You are her mother and you need to raise her, if I can help that happen, I will."

I stopped eating. This was so unexpected I asked for clarification. Lisa had little other information about the woman except to say, "You could tell she really had her life together."

This woman was willing to lay down her life, not for her friends but for two strangers. Why? She was orienting to a higher purpose. The woman was willing to die for posterity or the good of future generations. It was not even her direct posterity, but for the posterity of someone else. She wanted a little girl to be raised by her mother and if someone needed to die for it to happen, she was willing to be the one.

I suddenly felt involved in the story in a new way, and I was not sure why. As I was writing this journal entry, an insight came. In her willingness to die for Lisa and Keely, the woman was willing to die for my posterity. Without knowing me, the woman of higher purpose was willing to die for my granddaughter. This means she was willing to die for me.

I was not only grateful that Lisa and Keely were safe; I was also grateful for a stranger who was living for a higher purpose. Prior to our dinner conversation, I only knew of a story that I interpreted to be about the spreading evil in the world. After the dinner conversation, I knew a story I now interpreted to be about the profound good in the world. I am grateful for a stranger, a woman of purpose who really has her life together.

Often people "get their life together" because they have found a higher purpose or learned to live for a higher purpose. As we have seen, a purpose is higher when it transcends immediate self-interest, when you transition from a contract to a covenant. A higher purpose is a contributive goal, or what social scientists call a "prosocial goal," meaning the focus is on contributing to the good of the whole.

So living with a higher purpose is focusing on and sacrificing for something bigger than yourself. Research indicates that doing this leads to the development of the following personal characteristics: taking initiative, assisting others, persisting in meaningful tasks, being open to negative feedback, motivating others, stimulating new ideas, and inspiring creative action.[32] This is a reasonable list of leadership characteristics. As you begin to live a purpose-driven life, virtuous characteristics tend to ignite. You become a better version of yourself.

The woman who volunteered to die for Lisa and Keely demonstrated many of these qualities. In doing so, she was leading. Leaders with a higher purpose are focused on the common good. This transcendence of self-interest gives rise to moral power. Moral power is the influence that emanates from a person or persons who selflessly pursue the common good. As with selfishness, moral power is contagious, and it can spread. It draws attention and invites new behaviors. When people of authentic, higher purpose act, they tend to bring out the best in others. If they continue over time, they bring forth a high-performance culture.

Organizational Higher Purpose

An example of a focus on higher purpose comes from Eric Greitens, a former Navy Seal and governor of Missouri. Here is an excerpt from our interview with him:

> I believe that people can have very strong internal motivations that
> can drive them toward achievement. But I think that is related to

but different from your sense of purpose. Part of what you have
to do to help somebody to see their sense of purpose is to actually
communicate to them that they have something to offer. What
we're doing in many ways with our Mission Continues Fellows
is that we are asking them to serve. We're forcing them into a
situation where they then have to see that they have something to
contribute.

As a Navy Seal lieutenant commander, Eric was awarded a
Bronze Star and Purple Heart, among other decorations. Following
his military service, he founded The Mission Continues, a nonprofit
organization that helps reintegrate disabled war veterans into society. This is how Eric described the higher purpose of The Mission
Continues:

> Our mission is to challenge veterans to serve and lead in com-
> munities across America. That's our mission. We also have a
> purpose, which is to make it the case that every veteran who comes
> here thinks of their military service not in terms of the time when
> they were in the field. What's interesting is that these people have
> a sense of purpose from the beginning. Some veterans think of
> having a higher sense of purpose as being part of a team, being
> devoted to something larger than yourself, and something that
> they did in the military. We want to change that to something that
> they learned in the military and that they apply to the rest of their
> lives. . . . Our objective at The Mission Continues is to make sure
> that the story becomes one so that 10 years from now, people will
> look back on this generation and say that they came home and they
> continued to serve. They came home and they made their country
> stronger. So that's kind of our larger purpose.

After we interviewed Eric Greitens, he admitted to an extramari-
tal affair prior to becoming governor. He was investigated for having allegedly threatened the woman in question (prior to his public
admission) if she went public with that information, although no

complaint was ever filed by the woman. He subsequently resigned as governor of Missouri after only six months in office. Given this situation, we were advised to drop the example of The Mission Continues. Our response is that it is crucial to keep the example. All human beings are flawed. We feel it is crucial to keep the account presented here and for the reader to consider the notion that moral power is a dynamic phenomenon that ebbs and flows.

Another example of organizational higher purpose is provided by Walt Disney. On the pitch statement to obtain funding for the Disneyland park in California, Walt Disney wrote: "In these pages is proffered a glimpse into this great adventure—a preview of what the visitor will find in Disneyland."

Later in the pitch, Walt Disney articulated a higher purpose that has influenced the company's business strategy time and again:

> The idea of Disneyland is a simple one. It will be a place for people to find happiness and knowledge.
>
> It will be a place for parents and children to share pleasant times in one another's company: a place for teachers and pupils to discover greater ways of understanding and education. Here the older generation can recapture nostalgia of days gone by, and the younger generation can savor the challenge of the future. Here will be the wonders of Nature and Man for all to see and understand.
>
> Disneyland will be based upon and dedicated to the ideals, the dreams and hard facts that have created America. And it will be uniquely equipped to dramatize these dreams and facts and send them forth as a source of courage and inspiration to all the world.
>
> Disneyland will be something of a fair, an exhibition, a playground, a community center, a museum of living facts, and a showplace of beauty and magic.
>
> It will be filled with the accomplishments, the joys and hopes of the world we live in. And it will remind us and show us how to make those wonders part of our own lives.[33]

An Economic Theory of Higher Purpose

Our economic theory of higher purpose:

> The adoption of an authentic higher purpose creates a bond
> between employees and the purpose and motivates them to work
> harder, be more entrepreneurial, and subordinate their self-interest
> for the common good, all in order to help the organization serve
> its higher purpose. This results in better economic performance.
> However, these things happen only if employees believe that the
> purpose is authentic.

We begin our discussion of the theory with a simple observation:
a major purpose of a leader is to recognize the common good and
sacrifice for it so that others will follow.[34] We proceed to the following building block for an economic theory of higher purpose:

> Self-interested people will remain self-interested unless there is a
> reason to change. In a purpose-driven organization, leaders con-
> tinually orient to the common good and make personal sacrifices,
> and this unconventional behavior repels some but attracts others to
> do the same. Relationships change, and people at all levels begin to
> energize one another.

To use this building block and develop an economic theory, we
first put in place assumptions. The first assumption is that employees
care about two things—the pecuniary and nonpecuniary rewards
they receive from the organization for the job they do, and the utility they derive from pursuing a prosocial goal that transcends their
narrow self-interest. But many employees may be uncertain about
how much utility they derive from a particular prosocial goal or
organizational higher purpose, and also about *how* to integrate the
pursuit of higher purpose into their day-to-day business activities
and decisions. They may need to experiment and reflect to discover
this. If an employee believes that the organization has an authentic

higher purpose, then that employee will be willing to work harder than if the only motivation was the combination of pecuniary and nonpecuniary job rewards.

In other words, employees are willing to "sacrifice for the common good" because doing so provides them with satisfaction or utility beyond that provided by the wage and promotion rewards of working hard. Doing so serves as a covenant and generates utility-enhancing intrinsic rewards for the individual, something that does not happen when they are simply responding to a contract.

The key, of course, is that the employees must truly believe in the authenticity of the organizational pursuit of higher purpose. To create such belief, a leader must do the following:

➢ Discover and believe in an authentic higher purpose

➢ Communicate the higher purpose

➢ Integrate the authentic higher purpose with the business strategy

➢ Weave the authentic higher purpose into their execution of the strategy, that is, in their day-to-day decisions

The second assumption is that there are two kinds of leaders: those who authentically believe in a higher purpose ("true believers"), and those who are interested only in the pursuit of business goals but are willing to masquerade as true believers in order to get their employees to sacrifice for the common good and change their behavior ("manipulators").

Only leaders know their own types; to others they all look the same. Moreover, suppose the sacrifices made by employees in the pursuit of higher purpose produce better outcomes regardless of what the leader does, but these gains are small relative to those produced when the leader commits wholeheartedly to an authentic higher purpose and continues to behave over time in a manner consistent with the higher purpose.

Both types of leaders have an incentive to say that they are true believers. But the employees, even though they may not be able to always tell who is a true believer and who is not, know that the leaders have this incentive to masquerade as true believers. This means that the embrace of higher purpose by the leader of the organization will be viewed with suspicion by the employees, and the leader will have to make a special effort to convince employees of authenticity. This is true even if the manipulator behaves exactly like the true believer and makes (short-term) sacrifices that are costly to them personally and to the organization.

However, a leader who is a true believer will always derive greater personal satisfaction and utility from pursuing an organizational higher purpose than a leader who is a manipulator. Thus, the net cost to the leader of pursuing an organizational higher purpose is smaller if the leader is a true believer than if the leader is a manipulator. So the true believer may be able to figure out the degree of commitment to purpose that is desirable for the true believer but too high for the manipulator.

If there is such a commitment to a higher purpose, then the employees will observe it and believe that it is authentic. But in order to do this, the leader has to first *discover* the higher purpose, one that makes sense for the organization given its business context. There is no formula for what constitutes a great higher purpose.

The examples we have provided thus far illustrate the great variety of authentic higher purposes. For Starbucks, the higher purpose was to "provide a third place between work and home." For Eric Greitens of The Mission Continues, it was to reintegrate disabled veterans into society by instilling in them a sense that their service is larger than themselves and that they can pursue their passion while serving society away from the battlefield. For Walt Disney, it was to create "a place where people can find happiness and knowledge." Organizational higher purpose is as varied as organizations themselves.

But any leader's first step is to envision a purpose-driven workforce and discover a higher purpose for the organization, recognizing that this "noble cause"—as defined by Steve Jobs—can be anything prosocial but requires deep contemplation and discovery. This is not always easy. For example, we interviewed Jim Weddle, the CEO of Edward Jones, a large financial services company headquartered in St. Louis. He described to us a process that Peter Drucker took Edward Jones through to discover its higher purpose.

When they began, they described the purpose of the organization as making a profit. Drucker refused to accept that answer, asserting that profit was an outcome of the pursuit of a higher purpose. The question he asked was "Why does the organization exist?" After a painful discussion that went back and forth, the organization eventually discovered its higher purpose as helping their clients—individuals and families—make financial decisions to achieve their life goals, not just helping them make money but helping them achieve their lifetime financial goals. This is a higher purpose that is not distinct from the business of the company. Rather, it is an integral part of it and influences every aspect of how the company is run.

Once an organization discovers a higher purpose, the leaders have to understand that it cannot be a covenant unless it is authentic and employees are convinced that it is authentic. In other words, employees must believe that the leader is not a manipulator who is articulating a higher purpose as a public relations ploy.

Authentic leadership requires not only the appropriate personal and organizational financial sacrifices to signal authenticity but also *clear* and *constant* messages. You cannot assume that the employees will hear the leader the first time a higher purpose is communicated. The message has to be repeated over and over again, and its implications for business decisions and tradeoffs have to be continuously explored, debated, and explained.

Repeating the message will help employees internalize the higher purpose and believe in it, and it will stimulate each of them to learn how they can integrate the organization's higher purpose into their decisions and actions. In this process, higher purpose becomes an arbiter of all decisions. They find that complexity is reduced, and freedom is increased. They can make the right decisions without asking for direction because they know the highest intention of the organization.

This learning process can energize employees. As they begin to live in the space at the intersection of organizational higher purpose and business decisions, they begin to make personal sacrifices that help to further the common good, and they become ambassadors for the higher purpose. In this way, midlevel managers are turned into purpose-driven leaders. As a result, intrafirm competition and self-interested behavior decline. Employees perceive less uncertainty about how their fellow employees will behave, reducing what economists refer to as *strategic uncertainty*. The lower uncertainty and the commitment to purpose permit the organization to change the wage contracts it writes for its employees. The organization does not rely on the expectation that all of the employee's motivation will come from the explicit wage contracts they are offered. The organization has a higher purpose that substitutes partially for the high-powered incentives of explicit wage contracts that pay bonuses that increase steeply with output. The organization can shield its (risk-averse) employees from some of the risk associated with such contracts without worrying about employees shirking. Employees work harder and smarter not only because they will earn higher bonuses by doing so but because doing so will contribute to a higher purpose they believe in.

Over time, these purpose-driven leaders begin to connect others in the organization to the higher purpose. Employees begin to see their work as not only helping the organization achieve its business goals but as something larger than themselves. The covenant begins to take hold. Like the war veterans in The Mission Continues, employees see themselves as making large contributions to society. Leading this charge of connecting people to purpose will be the *positive energizers*—those whose boundless enthusiasm for the higher purpose radiates brightly and converts others. Leaders must make sure these positive energizers are unleashed.

Thus, our theory of higher purpose does not seek to negate the principal–agent model but to augment it. We recognize the power of incentives in overcoming effort aversion and the extent to which employee risk aversion impedes contractual resolutions. An authentic organizational higher purpose reduces the risk employees perceive, and it also helps overcome employee aversion to working hard.

Economics of Higher Purpose at Work in Practice: A Case Study

We can see how organizations that do what we described above behave, especially during times of stress. One of these organizations is Southwest Airlines.

Southwest Airlines has long been known as a purpose-driven, values-based organization.[35] Pursuing the purpose and living the values often leads to unconventional decisions and positive outcomes. The 2001 attack on the World Trade Center had a devastating effect on air travel. As passengers turned away, airlines were forced to downsize, and many did so with a purely economic mind-set. US Airways, for example, declared financial exigency. This allowed it to lay off more employees than any other airline, with no benefits and no severance for the laid-off employees, as union contracts became null and void.

Like US Airways, Southwest was also a short-haul airline, and such airlines were the most adversely affected. However, Southwest acted on the assumption that the trust and loyalty of employees was more important than responding to short-term financial pressures. Southwest risked being severely punished by investors for not making the right economic decision. Yet over the next 12 months, while all airlines, including Southwest, had negative stock returns, Southwest's shareholders suffered the least among all major airlines. Southwest recovered more quickly that most of the other airlines.[36]

Southwest retains its ability to perform under pressure. In April 2018 Southwest experienced a different kind of crisis: a passenger was killed when pieces of a failed engine damaged the wing and the fuselage of a plane.[37] The airline faced many technical, legal, and financial issues, as well as issues of dealing with the grieving family and the 148 others who were on the plane.

Employees across the country rushed to respond, but in a crisis a workforce cannot be managed centrally. While a few basic directives can be sent out, hundreds of decisions have to be made in each location, without direction from above. At such times the culture reigns, and, as we know, some companies have failed miserably.

Southwest had two chief concerns: ensuring the safety of the rest of the fleet and caring for the affected customers. The company arranged a special flight, staffed by experienced crew, for the 148 passengers. The passengers later described the company as "friendly, understanding, concerned." Afterward, employees stayed in contact with the passengers. The company sent $5,000 to each passenger for immediate expenses. It sent the money in a letter from the CEO offering "our sincerest apologies."

The Southwest community felt sadness over the loss. Employees sent messages of compassion and support to one another and regularly checked on and cared for one another. As a former HR employee stated, "It's a different culture. When there's an issue, everybody feels it."

Empirical Evidence on the Economics of Higher Purpose

Recent research provides evidence to support the observation that pursuit of an authentic higher purpose improves economic performance. Two Swedish economists studied the effect of higher purpose pursuit in a laboratory study of principals and agents. They hypothesized that the pursuit of an authentic higher purpose creates in employees a "warm glow" about the firm, thereby positively influencing employee behavior. In a laboratory setting in which some participants in the experiment acted as principals and others as agents, they asked the principals in the treatment group to donate their earnings to the Swedish Red Cross in the various treatments designed in the experiment. They found that agents work the hardest and economic efficiency is the highest in the treatment in which a portion of the principal's earnings goes to charity. They concluded that the pursuit of higher purpose improves the efficacy of the contracts that principals and agents negotiate, and that this plays an important role in the higher effort agents provide.[38]

As we indicated in our economic theory of higher purpose in chapter 4, behavior can be significantly influenced by the pursuit of higher purpose in part because even the explicit contracts that are negotiated may be affected by this pursuit. In other words, it is the *entire ecosystem* of contracts, effort, and output that is fundamentally altered.

A large-sample study by researchers at Harvard Business School, Columbia University, and the Wharton School surveyed nearly 500,000 people across 429 firms involving 917 firm-year observations from 2006 to 2011. The study found that an authentic higher purpose that is communicated with clarity has a positive impact on both operating financial performance and forward-looking measures of performance like stock price.[39]

The authors found that high-purpose organizations come in two forms: firms characterized by high camaraderie between workers, and those characterized by high clarity from management. They document that firms exhibiting *both* higher purpose and clarity have systematically higher future earnings and stock market performance, even after controlling for current performance. They concluded that this relationship is driven by the perceptions of middle management and professional staff, rather than senior executives. Their findings are consistent with our economic theory of higher purpose: when midlevel employees believe that the organizational higher purpose is authentic and is communicated with clarity by top management, better economic performance results.

A study looked at the issue in the context of reward-based crowdfunding, in which creators of entrepreneurial projects solicit capital from potential *consumers* to reach a funding goal and offer them future products or services in return. The study examined consumers' contribution patterns using a novel dataset of 28,591 projects collected at 30-minute resolution from Kickstarter.com.[40] It showed that consumers also have prosocial motives to help creators reach their funding goals. Projects were funded faster right before they met their funding goals than right after, presumably because consumers wanted to direct more funds to projects that needed to successfully finish their funding campaigns so they could commence pursuit of their prosocial goals. These findings suggest that consumers' prosocial motives play a role in rewards-based crowdfunding.

Another study looked at an economic model of an industry equilibrium in which firms have a choice to engage in corporate social responsibility (CSR) activities.[41] The CSR is modeled as an investment to increase product differentiation that allows firms to benefit from higher profit margins, so there is an integration of higher purpose with the business goals of the company. The model predicts that CSR decreases systematic risk and increases firm value, and that these effects are stronger for firms with high product differentiation. The authors found supporting empirical evidence for these predictions.

Conclusion

In a nutshell, our economic theory of higher purpose is as follows: By adopting an authentic higher purpose that intersects the organization's business goals, employees are persuaded that their personally-costly effort has two effects—it contributes to their own economic well-being (through higher compensation, promotions, and other extrinsic rewards), and it contributes to a greater social good that they care about. This increases the value they perceive in their own hard work, making them willing to work harder, take more risks, and be more entrepreneurial than they would be otherwise. Thus, the power of extrinsic reward and punishment mechanisms in aligning the self-interest of employees with the larger good of the organization is enhanced. The key is that the economic sacrifice made by the authentic leader to pursue higher purpose must be great enough to convince employees that the purpose is authentic and not simply another tool to control and manipulate employees.

If higher purpose is so compelling, why is everybody not embracing it? We turn to this question in the next chapter.

CHAPTER SIX

Why Isn't Everyone Doing It?

We are not the first to elucidate the meaning of higher purpose. Indeed, a large number of books have been written on the subject, some on the role of higher purpose in the lives of individuals and others on the role of higher purpose in organizations. Authors talk about "leading with the soul," "managing from the outside in," "focusing first on the 'why' instead of the 'how.'" Yet few organizations have adopted an *authentic* higher purpose that influences their daily business decisions. Why? Why have the books had so little influence on actual business practice?

The Economic Case for Higher Purpose: The Threat to Free-Market Capitalism

This question is important because of the enormous potential that higher purpose has to change the world. Global corporations and market-driven capitalism have contributed handsomely to economic growth since World War II. This growth has significantly reduced poverty around the world. However, not everyone has benefited equally. Economic inequality has actually increased as a small fraction of the population has benefited more than the rest. The situation is worse in developing countries.[42]

This failure to spread the wealth equally has led to a disillusionment with capitalism in many quarters. A recent Gallup survey of Americans found that, for the first time, the percentage of Democrats favoring socialism was higher than that favoring capitalism. While a much lower percentage of Republicans like socialism (16 percent), in 2018 a majority of Americans ages 18 to 29 had a more favorable view of socialism (51 percent) than of capitalism (45 percent).[43]

For those who believe in free markets and are aware of all the evidence of failed experiments in socialism, this result is shocking. It is an existential threat to the very economic system that underlies much of the prosperity enjoyed by the West in the decades since World War II and the rapidly growing prosperity in emerging market countries. Rather than dismissing these attitudes favoring socialism as stemming from a lack of information, a misunderstanding of what socialism really is, or political ideology, we can ponder how capitalism can deal with this challenge in a way that restores faith in the capitalist economic system. We believe that one way to restore faith in the system is for corporations to adopt authentic prosocial higher purposes, without government coaxing or societal pressure.[44] If firms fail to do so, the consequences will be dire. We are all acutely aware of instances in which voters get so dissatisfied with the status quo that they vote in favor of something even worse.

This disillusionment has happened despite an increasing focus on corporate programs that are often linked to corporate higher purpose. Indeed, corporate social responsibility (CSR) programs can often provide valuable ideas for corporations to discover their higher purpose. An example of such a CSR program is Syngenta's Good Growth Plan, which aims to increase the productivity of small farmers in Indonesia and Nicaragua. Yet many of these programs have failed to deliver the promised results.

Robert Kaplan, George Serafeim, and Edward Tugendhat surmise that this failure is due to companies undertaking insufficiently ambitious programs. They propose that "instead of trying to fix local problems, corporations and other actors need to reimagine the regional ecosystems in which they participate if they are to bring poor farmers and unemployed urban youths into the mainstream economy."[45]

They propose that companies should search for projects that generate economic benefits for the companies themselves while creating socioeconomic gains for others in the "new ecosystem" created by their investments. Such projects require investments from a diversified group of other players and can potentially scale up to other communities and regions.

Kaplan and colleagues provide an example from Uganda, where Carana Corporation, a global economic-development consultancy firm, started a project in 2010 to create a supply chain to bring small and poor Ugandan maize farmers into the mainstream regional economy. The authors describe the project:

> This required deep engagement with multiple players, including Nile Breweries, grain traders, and the farmers themselves. It involved multiple investments in new assets and capabilities for the traders and farmers, including the creation of maize demonstration plots to showcase good agricultural practices and proper postharvest handling techniques. An offtake agreement with Nile Breweries facilitated farmers' access to credit and attracted input suppliers that could help farmers finance the purchase of improved seeds, equipment, and fertilizers along with access to irrigation and pest- and fungus-control solutions.

By 2015 the new supply chain included 27,000 farmers, with more than half of them being female. The farmers' median crop yields rose by 65 percent, household incomes more than doubled, and participating farmers' net incomes increased by 50 percent. Farmers' families experienced a dramatic improvement in their diets, and farmers began to purchase drought-resistant seeds and crop insurance. Numerous other effects rippled through the economy as more and more companies entered the region to create a "sustainable mass for an agribusiness cluster."

The project also improved the quality of life. One farmer said, "Things are different now. All my children own pairs of shoes. We are a happy family that can afford to eat meat and chicken, which were unheard of in my home before. My children enjoy school because they no longer feel left out."

The advice that Kaplan and colleagues offer is for companies to aim for higher organizational purpose of this sort. Will companies take it? We hope so. However, in this chapter we explain why many companies may not, despite the enormous potential that they might realize.

The Economics of the Failure to Adopt an Authentic Higher Purpose

We can look to our economic theory of higher purpose that was developed in chapter 5 for an answer. To see the answer, suppose that times are normal and our firm is doing quite well. The employees are being well paid, customers want the firm's products and services, and investors are earning rates of return that are high enough to compensate them for risk and the time value of money.

We said in chapter 5 that in order to establish authenticity, the leader who is a true believer has to make a commitment to the organization's higher purpose that is big enough to keep manipulators from mimicking it. The manipulators are deterred because they perceive a smaller marginal benefit from the higher purpose and hence a higher net marginal cost from pursuing it. That is, the manipulators see the personal and organizational cost of pursuing a higher purpose, but they assess that the personal and organizational cost is so small that it does not seem worth pursuing. When times are good, two things happen. First, investing financial and other resources in the pursuit of higher purpose is not particularly costly because the investment is "affordable." So both the true believer and the manipulator can afford to invest large amounts of resources in it.

Second, the marginal value of the pursuit of higher purpose is also relatively small during the good times. Economists view people as having diminishing marginal utility of consumption. This means that you value an extra unit of wealth or consumption less when you are well off than when you are not doing so well. So whatever the firm does in the pursuit of higher purpose is valued less by those—customers or employees—who benefit from it.

In the Southwest Airlines example we discussed in chapter 5, if Southwest had committed to not laying off any people as an illustration of the practice of its higher purpose during good times, any other airline could have imitated it because no airline wanted to lay people off anyway. An airline would have incurred no economic sacrifice in committing to this course of action. The action also would have been less meaningful to employees since they would have known that the company was not going to lay them off anyway, and even if it did, it is easy to find another job when the economy is doing well.

But the situation changes during a crisis. After 9/11 Southwest was losing $5 million per day, so not laying off any employees meant a major economic sacrifice. Other airlines found mimicking Southwest very costly, making Southwest's commitment authentic and credible. Moreover, facing an industry downturn in which finding another job would have been difficult for employees, Southwest's decision not to lay off any employees had especially high value to employees.

Because of these two effects, for any given resource committed to higher purpose, the net perceived cost of pursuing higher purpose is not that much greater for the manipulator than it is for the true believer when times are good. This result makes it more difficult for the true believer to separate from the manipulator by ensuring that the manipulator will not mimic the true believer. Indeed, the resource commitment to the higher purpose may call for such a big financial sacrifice that investors may be unwilling to tolerate it. Even a leader who is a true believer may find that they are boxed in and unable to pursue the higher purpose.

Another factor that may discourage the adoption of higher purpose during good times is that a manipulator may have pet projects that generate personal utility but have few prosocial benefits. These pet projects may destroy significant shareholder value.[46] For example, a CEO who has political ambitions decides to give away products or services to certain constituent groups—in the name of the pursuit of higher purpose—in order to curry political goodwill for a future run for office. Or a CEO may undertake activities that help them develop a reputation for generosity in order to get more seats on corporate boards of directors. In such cases, the manipulator may perceive a high personal benefit from allocating substantial organizational resources to the pursuit of the activity that requires financial sacrifices by the company. The activity would be dressed up to look like a higher purpose, and a sufficiently large commitment of organizational resources may even make it appear authentic to employees. The manipulator would be willing to make the large commitment because they would perceive a relatively low *net* marginal cost of doing so due to the high personal benefit.

Just like employees, investors may be unable to distinguish between a manipulator and a true believer. But they would rationally recognize the possibility. This recognition may lead them to be suspicious of *all* pursuits of higher purpose. So investor activism may obstruct the pursuit of higher purpose.

Indeed, this suspicion is an important reason why economists like Milton Friedman and many others so strongly advocate shareholder value maximization as the main goal that companies should pursue. The goal is for the wealth of the firm's owners to be maximized after the claims of all others have been satisfied. It leaves no room for the pursuit of pet projects. No one has to figure out whether the CEO is pursuing a pet project to the detriment of the firm or a prosocial goal to benefit society. It has clarity. It means that you maximize the value of the residual claims of the firm's owners. This clarity provides the discipline needed to ensure that resources are not mismanaged.

The introduction of higher purpose complicates the picture. Leaders look not only for opportunities that maximize shareholder value (in the long run), but also those that serve an authentic higher purpose: the intersection of higher purpose and business purpose. But the bigger the distance between the company's operations and the higher purpose it articulates, the more daunting is the task of convincing investors and employees that the higher purpose is authentic. Thus, the higher purpose of developing ambitious programs like regional ecosystems may prove quite formidable for many companies to adopt.

The Effect of a Crisis

When there is a crisis, things change. Any financial sacrifice made by the firm or personal sacrifice made by the leader becomes significantly more costly to both the true believer and the manipulator. But the manipulator has a smaller perceived benefit than the true believer. More importantly, the difference between the true believer and the manipulator in terms of their calculations of the perceived marginal benefit of pursuing the higher purpose may be much bigger during a crisis than during normal times. The easiest way to see this is to make the extreme assumption that the manipulator attaches *no* value to the pursuit of higher purpose. In that case, the marginal value of the higher purpose pursuit is greater for the true believer during a crisis than during normal times, so the *difference* between the manipulator and the true believer in terms of their *net* costs of pursuing the higher purpose is also greater during a crisis. This difference enables the true believer to adopt a higher purpose in a way that deters mimicry by the manipulator.

What about a manipulator pursuing a pet project masquerading as a pursuit of higher purpose? Two considerations make this very difficult during a crisis. First, the commitment of resources to the pet project can put the survival of the organization at risk. Imagine Ricardo and the pain caused by the downsizing that was essential for survival. This may be a cost that a leader who is not a true believer may be unwilling to bear. Second, financiers are likely to be more inquisitive and willing to invest more resources into investigating the leader's pursuit of the so-called higher purpose during a period of crisis. There is simply more at stake. This scrutiny may increase the likelihood of the pet project being exposed for what it truly is during a crisis to such an extent that the manipulator is simply unwilling to risk it.

The anticipated behavior of the manipulator also affects the true believer. A leader who is a true believer can adopt a higher purpose without worrying so much about mimicry by a manipulator. They can pursue that higher purpose without risking everything, although in many instances in which a higher purpose emerges from a crisis, the commitment of resources to the higher purpose is substantial.

Thus, the pursuit of higher purpose often arises during crises because it is, perhaps surprisingly, easier for the leader to convey authenticity and convince employees that they will continue to pursue the higher purpose. A covenant, like the one described by Ricardo and Rabbi Sacks, often emerges during a crisis because it unites people more readily to a common purpose they must sacrifice for. Moreover, the recipients of the benefits of the pursuit of higher purpose value the benefits very highly. Consequently, the beliefs of employees about the future change, and a profound change in behavior emerges.

More on Higher Purpose and Crisis

When people experience a life trauma, the conventional response is to become stressed and depressed. The way out is to clarify and articulate one's highest purpose. Purpose shifts the focus from a sense of loss to the value of loss in teaching us how to move forward. Purpose gives rise to learning, renewal, and regeneration.

An interesting interaction takes place between a crisis (which is an exogenous shock), higher purpose, and the behavior people exhibit during the crisis. We have discovered that this interaction is a recurring theme. In our workshops we often give participants the opportunity to reexamine their lives by telling their most important stories. When we do this, one theme overshadows all the others. The participants speak of a crisis, how it tested them, how they got through it, and the positive benefits they now see. So while we have discussed how a higher purpose emerges from a crisis, we then turn to how having a higher purpose helps you cope with a crisis.

Our colleague Vic Strecher has a chapter in his book on purpose, challenge, and learning.[47] He suggests that having a life purpose greatly influences how you respond in times of difficulty. If you have a purpose, you think differently than you would otherwise. You have greater consciousness, and you exercise more control on how you construct meaning from your experience. Over time, you learn to think about how you think, and you learn to control how you think. You learn to invest your energy in your desired future.

Strecher reviews studies of responses to devastating earthquakes. After an earthquake, many people suffer for long periods. However, people with a life purpose are less likely to suffer from stress, depression, and lower quality of life. They are more likely to learn and grow from their traumatic experience and live a higher-quality life. They experience more growth, are less likely to suffer from traumatic stress, and have more energy and will power. In fact, the more extensive the crisis, the greater the post-traumatic growth.

These findings suggest that when you have a purpose and experience great challenges, you put less focus on what is lost and more focus on your purpose. Pursuing the purpose keeps you moving forward. Moving forward reduces your sense of fear. It promotes confidence and learning. The learning is not conventional but deep, transformative learning. You come to a new view of who you are and how you can act upon the world.

Challenge opens you up. In times of challenge, you have to reexamine your values, assumptions and perceptions. You have to take a fresh view, one centered in the present reality not in past experiences. As you go through this process, if you did not previously have a purpose, you gain one. If you did have a purpose, you test and clarify it. You thus "repurpose" your life.

As you experience stressors in life, you tend to respond with bitterness (fight) or denial (flight). But a healthier response is to accept reality and adapt. You are able to engage in this kind of learning more easily when you have a life purpose and you live in hope of a better future. Our economic theory of authentic higher purpose suggests that people can become leaders who create high-performance organizations. While this often happens through crisis, that is not always the case; each person can take charge of their own leadership development.

The Personal Challenge in Adopting Higher Purpose

Our work has revealed numerous reasons why executives fail to adopt a higher purpose for their organizations. The following lists are the six central challenges they face. The bullet points reflect some of the responses of 44 executives from a Fortune 500 company when we asked them to share their most authentic personal question regarding leading change.

Personal Doubt

➤ What if I am not sure I am the right person to lead the change?

➤ How do I lead strategic change when my orientation and my role are anchored in control?

➤ How do I help my team believe that the impossible is possible?

➤ How do I get people with no sense of ownership to believe they can create change?

➢ How do I motivate my team to provide innovative services when morale is low, bonus payouts are declining, and attrition is increasing?

➢ How do I inspire folks to enter troubled waters where they need to move back and forth between collaboration and competition?

➢ How can I become someone who, like a monk, unselfishly helps others?

Dealing with personal doubt. If you have doubts about whether you are the right person to lead, much of it can be dissipated by joining others in the organization to discover the purpose. We explain how to do this in chapters 7 and 8.

Ethical Conflict

➢ What if I am not sure I *want* to invest in the change? What if I genuinely think the change is not good for the team?

➢ How do I inspire others to make a change when I am not authentically committed?

➢ How do I realign my team's goals and execution when my team's original charter may get shot down during reorganization?

➢ How do I live every day—and make decisions based on—what I truly believe instead of what I think I am supposed to believe and do?

Dealing with personal doubt and ethical conflict. If you are personally unsure of your own authentic commitment to the higher purpose, don't do it. Either you need to do more contemplation to determine if the purpose is right for you, or you need to move on to discovering a purpose that you can believe in. Just remember that if you are looking for reassurance or proof that the chosen higher purpose will "work," you are not going to find it. You will see the power of the purpose only if you believe in it. In other words, you will have to believe in it first before you will see its power.

Time Stress

➤ How do I create change when I have only enough time for the next customer crisis?

➤ How can I maintain work-life balance?

➤ How do I balance being a senior leader and with having time for my family?

Dealing with time stress. Time stress is a big issue for many, but it is not something that is going to go away. However, if you feel passionate about the higher purpose, creativity will follow, and you will come up with a creative solution to the problem of not having enough time. Indeed, clarifying your highest purpose is transformational because it becomes the arbiter of all decisions. When you know your highest purpose, many things that otherwise keep you busy begin to drop off your to-do list. Things you thought you had to do are no longer the right things to do.

Horizontal Distrust

➤ How do I get peers who want to dominate and defeat others to want to collaborate and cooperate with others?

➤ How do I inspire my team and peers to collaborate without being blocked by the question "What is in it for me?"

➤ How do I ensure transparency across the business in the face of so many competing and short-term pressures coming at me from others?

➤ How can I learn to excel in this competitive world?

Dealing with horizontal distrust. There is only one way to overcome the very real challenge of horizontal distrust—turn your midlevel managers into purpose-driven leaders and then unleash the positive energizers. They will help you deal with those who may generate horizontal distrust. We address how to deal with this challenge in chapter 12.

Vertical Misalignment

➢ How do I know if I can I change the culture when I am not on top of the hierarchy and am led by someone who does not like to be challenged?

➢ How do I implement a higher purpose when I am not given control?

➢ Do I have the courage and skill to influence my management to implement the organizational changes I believe necessary when they do not want the change?

➢ How do I save a business unit that, because of selfish decisions by our top executives and a lack of leadership, is going to suffer layoffs, missed targets, a disengaged salesforce, and another reorganization?

➢ How do I get my team to think long term when the management above me thinks only short term (we step over $100 bills to pick up $1 bills)?

Cultural Expectations

➢ How do I promote collaboration in a company that does not value it and with an executive level that is not really committed to it?

➢ How do I respond to the need to move faster in a risk-averse culture?

➢ How do I lead change when competing tasks and initiatives are pulling the culture in another direction?

➢ How do I remain passionate when surrounded by mediocrity?

➢ Can I have a big enough impact on improving the culture on a large scale to keep me working for this company?

Dealing with vertical misalignment and cultural expectations. These seem like unresolvable issues. We normally assume that organizational culture comes from the top and cascades down the organization. The boss is an impossible barrier. This assumption prevents the emergence of proactive leadership at every level. Yet we often find middle managers who have created purpose-driven, positive units in the midst of conventional hierarchies. These few are the real leaders. Authority figures, from top to bottom, who operate from conventional assumptions do not create purpose-driven organizations. Yet in most large systems, there are a small minority of leaders who do create them. All the steps in chapters 7 to 14 will help you think about how to do this.

PART II

Eight Steps for Creating the Purpose-Driven Organization

I n part 2, chapters 7 through 15, we turn to the question of how you create a purpose-driven organization. We guide you through eight steps for creating an organization of higher purpose.

STEP 1, in chapter 7, is to envision the organization of higher purpose. When you believe that your workforce can become purpose driven, you can envision what that organization might look like.

STEP 2, in chapter 8, is to discover the purpose. Once you believe that the organization can become purpose driven, you must understand the process by which purpose comes into consciousness.

STEP 3, in chapter 9, is to meet the need for authenticity. You have to make sure that the higher purpose is genuine and that you believe in it and are willing to sacrifice for it.

STEP 4, in chapter 10, is to turn the purpose constant. You can change the culture by making the higher purpose the arbiter of all decisions. You can make it part of the DNA of the organization.

STEP 5, in chapter 11, is to stimulate individual learning. When you create a purpose-driven organization, learning accelerates. Employees learn and grow as they figure out innovative ways to change the way the work is done. Everyone wins.

STEP 6, in chapter 12, is to turn the midlevel managers into purpose-driven leaders. When the people of the middle layers become purpose driven, the entire culture becomes change ready.

STEP 7, in chapter 13, is to connect people to the purpose. When people embrace purpose at every level, change readiness becomes change.

STEP 8, in chapter 14, is to unleash the positive energizers. When you identify and then enlist the positive energizers who believe in the purpose and can spread it rapidly throughout the organization, they turbocharge the implementation of the higher purpose.

CHAPTER SEVEN

STEP 1 Envision the Purpose-Driven Organization

For years our friend Horst Abraham has made a practice of visiting inmates in prison. He was surprised to learn that the prisoners he has visited were less likely to return to prison than prisoners in formal recovery programs. We asked him, "Why do they do better?"

In responding to this question, he told us he sees prisoners as human beings who are full of potential. To help us understand, he shared a note he received from one of the men he visits.

> I don't know whether you know, I always look forward to my contact with you. It is a lifeline. I look forward to take pen to paper and write to you, as I know you are listening. Your replies are consistently "more questions," not advice such as we get plenty of from prison guards, counselors and clergy, just curious questions. Our exchange makes me think about life and its greater meaning beyond these walls, thought walls that are even more confining than the cement walls. Thanks for being my pen pal. Your writing provides me with "oxygen."

Thought Walls

We are all prisoners. We are confined within our "thought walls." We each have a set of beliefs we have accumulated from experience. In this book we refer to these beliefs or assumptions as "the conventional mind-set." The conventional mind-set leads authority figures to give advice. People of purpose, like Horst, tend to let go of the expert role. They seek to inspire learning and nurture the rise of meaning. Success in the endeavor leads to empowerment and freedom from one's own thought walls.

Two things can challenge and pull us out of the conventional mind-set. One is crisis and the other is the choice to reflect on experience in a disciplined way. Horst helps people make the latter choice.

One way to change perception so people can see beyond thought walls is to expose them to positive exceptions to the rule. Consider this July 2015 blog post by Mike Rowe, host of the Discovery Channel show *Dirty Jobs*, about an experience he had at a Hampton Inn:

> I left my hotel room this morning to jump out of a perfectly good airplane, and saw part of a man standing in the hallway. His feet were on a ladder. The rest of him was somewhere in the ceiling.
>
> I introduced myself, and asked what he [was] doing. Along with satisfying my natural curiosity, it seemed a good way to delay my appointment with gravity, which I was in no hurry to keep. His name is Corey Mundle. . . . We quickly got to talking.
>
> "Well Mike, here's the problem," he said. "My pipe has a crack in it, and now my hot water is leaking into my laundry room. I've got to turn off my water, replace my old pipe, and get my new one installed before my customers notice there's a problem."
>
> I asked if he needed a hand, and he told me the job wasn't dirty enough. We laughed, and Corey asked if he could have a quick photo. I said sure, assuming he'd return the favor. He asked why I wanted a photo of him, and I said it was because I liked his choice of pronouns.
>
> "I like the way you talk about your work," I said. "It's not, 'the' hot water, it's 'MY' hot water. It's not, 'the' laundry room, it's 'MY'

laundry room. It's not 'a' new pipe, it's 'MY' new pipe. Most people don't talk like that about their work. Most people don't own it."

Corey shrugged and said, "This is not 'a' job; this is 'MY' job. I'm glad to have it, and I take pride in everything I do."

He didn't know it, but Corey's words made my job a little easier that day. Because three hours later, when I was trying to work up the courage to leap out of a perfectly good airplane, I wasn't thinking about pulling the ripcord on the parachute—I was thinking about pulling MY ripcord. On MY parachute.[48]

Corey Mundle is a purpose-driven employee. Instead of minimizing effort like the typical agent, he takes ownership. The fact that he and other people like him exist is important. When we're coaching executives on how to do purpose work in their organizations, we often tell them, "If it is real, it is possible." If you can find one positive example—a person, a team, a unit, that exceeds the norms—you can create a sense of hope by helping people examine the excellence that already exists. Look for excellence. Examine the purpose that drives the excellence. Then imagine a purpose-driven workforce.

When we learn to do as the prisoner did and "think about life and its greater meaning," we increase in understanding. We often acquire a sense of purpose. As we pursue a higher purpose, we open up to feedback. As we move forward shaping the future, we begin to discard old beliefs. As we grow, we gain a sense of empowerment. Like the prisoner, we begin to feel free.

One purpose of this book is to invite the reader to take a more inclusive view of organizations and leadership and ponder how to create a purpose-driven organization. So in each chapter in part 2 we state a conventional assumption and follow it with an assumption from the inclusive perspective and a counterintuitive step for building an organization of higher purpose. The first step is: Envision the purpose-driven organization.

Breaking Down Thought Walls

We recently had a collective experience like the individual experience reported by Horst. We worked with a major company that tends to have a narrow focus on profit. Managers tend to be cynical. In the first day of a leadership program, we introduced the executives to higher purpose and the acquisition of the inclusive, positive lens. They were not buying it.

They shared arguments of learned helplessness. It became apparent that the thought walls were thick. They told us, "The culture is determined from the top. I can't do anything about it." They also said, "We can only respond to the culture. There is no opportunity to exercise positive leadership in a top-down company."

The Power of Inquiry

We asked them to do an exercise. We divided them into four groups and gave each group a question:

➤ What is the difference between a good conversation and a great conversation?

➤ What is the difference between a good marriage and a great marriage?

➤ What is the difference between a good team and a great team?

➤ What is the difference between a good organization and a great organization?

We gave the groups time to discuss their experiences and asked each group to make a list that answered their given question. Here are their answers:

What is the difference between a good conversation and a great conversation?

➤ Both people are completely engaged and present.

➤ The conversation is highly energized.

➢ Both parties feel emotionally and intellectually stimulated.

➢ There is a sense of mutual inspiration, discovery, and creation.

➢ Each person leaves with more than they brought.

➢ The memory is vivid, and there is a desire for more.

What is the difference between a good marriage and a great marriage?

➢ The relationship is rich.

➢ There is mindfulness and attention to little things that create respect, empathy, and trust.

➢ There is mutual understanding and oneness; there is a mind meld.

➢ Conflicts are resolvable.

➢ Partners operate around shared values.

➢ Both partners are continually growing.

What is the difference between a good team and a great team?

➢ There is a shared purpose or vision.

➢ Team members feel challenged and engaged. They even challenge themselves.

➢ Team members are passionate.

➢ There is diversity, but it is integrated.

➢ Trust and collaboration are high.

➢ Team members enjoy doing what they do.

➢ There is a sense of high achievement.

➢ There is impact beyond the immediate team.

What is the difference between a good organization and a great organization?

➢ There is deep purpose in the existence of the organization.

➢ The intent is shared.

➢ The people willingly contribute their energy.

➢ There is synergy. The organization is greater than the sum of the parts.

➢ There is continual learning, adaptation, and innovation.

➢ There is a sense of impact and success.

➢ The organization develops an extra dimension; it becomes a magnet that attracts resources.

An Emergent Vision

We congratulated the executives on their thoughtful responses. We then asked them to look at the four lists they had constructed and create a new list. We asked, What does excellence look like in any social system? After much discussion they proposed the following:

➢ A higher purpose emerges.

➢ The people become committed to shared values.

➢ The people become energized, fully engaged, and they want to contribute.

➢ There is integrity.

➢ There is respect, and the people begin to trust each other.

➢ Egos fall off and conversations are more honest, vulnerable, and authentic.

➢ Mutuality increases. Everyone shares and everyone is heard.

➢ Ideas are built on one another.

➢ Conversations become both passionate and logical; they are inspirational and generative.

➢ Individual differences are integrated, and the sharing becomes synergistic.

➢ The conversations produce new resources.

➢ Learning becomes constant. Individuals and relationships are growing and evolving.

➢ Potential is actualized.

➢ Outcomes exceed expectations.

➢ The results matter; there is a culture of success.

➢ The success breeds success, it is inspiring, and it attracts new resources.

We asked the executives if they believed in their theory of excellence. They said they did. We told them that their theory was an emergent vision. We asked them where their vision came from. Had we given it to them? They said no—they had collectively drawn on their experiences and on their mutual discussions of those experiences.

We asked the executives to identify the implications of what they had just created.

They paused, and then a golden moment unfolded. They recognized, despite all their statements of helplessness and disbelief, that social excellence emerges from time to time in a variety of settings. It emerges often enough they could even describe it.

We asked the executives if excellence is attractive. Would they like to live in great conversations, great marriages, great teams, and great organizations? They replied in the affirmative. We told them that if excellence is real, that is, if it occurs in the world, excellence is possible. So the question is, How do you create excellence in any context, including their conversations, marriages, teams, and organizations?

Creating Excellence

We told them that two things tend to bring about social excellence. One is crisis and the other is genuine leadership. Not management, but leadership. This statement was painful. It suggested they were not leading.

A quiet woman raised her hand. She timidly told us that her unit had all the characteristics of excellence. We pressed her for details, and she told an impressive tale about her unit. We asked the group if they believed her. After all, everyone knew it was impossible to create excellence in their harsh, top-down company.

Two others came forward with similar claims. We asked for insights. One of the two said, "Creating a positive, purpose-driven unit is hard, but the payoffs are high; everyone wins. Why lead in any other way?"

This strongly expressed, unexpected statement brought a thoughtful silence. The group had come a long way from their initial statements of helplessness. Like the prisoner, they were breaking down their own thought walls. We were preparing them to envision and create a positive, purpose-driven organization.

A Visioning Exercise

In workshops, participants often ask something like this: "In practical terms, what is a positive, purpose-driven organization?" We no longer answer. Instead, we invite them to create their own vision. We put them through the following brief exercise. You may find it helpful.

We ask people to think about their organization as a dynamic system that ebbs and flows over time. We then ask them to focus not on the typical points but on one of the most extreme points: "What is your organization like when it is at its best? Please write some key words."

With their list in hand, they examine the checklist that appears in the Getting Started section at the end of this chapter. They then identify any phrase or word that they want to add to their existing list of key words.

With their expanded list in mind, they write their own vision of what their unit might look like if it was functioning at full potential. We emphasize that they should write only what they believe is possible, and they should write it in a language that can be understood by all. They then write a strategy that might turn their unit into a positive, purpose-driven organization.

The process of writing tends to have high impact. The participants create an unconventional image that they find believable. The process shifts their minds from what cannot be done to what they believe can be done. They end up inspiring themselves. As one participant said, "Writing this changes everything. I want to try some things I've never before imagined."

In some programs, we spend an entire week exploring how to create a positive, purpose-driven organization. In the example of the group we worked with, the group came to an inspiring outcome.

As the participants were sharing their insights, a man raised his hand. He said, "I am going to say something I never thought I would say. I came into this week genuinely pissed off at the senior leaders of this company. Now my anger is gone. I realize that they do not matter. Regardless of how they act, I can lead. I can clarify our highest purpose and create a positive organization, and that is what I am going to do."

There was silence in the room. This executive had just become the voice of a subset of the group. He did not express the voice of helplessness. Some of the executives were now seeing beyond their own thought walls. They were envisioning the purpose-driven organization. Bob walked over and gave this man a high five.

Summary

The principal–agent model focuses on the role of explicit contracts, and organizations spend a great deal of time and money in designing incentive contracts to produce the desired behavior by their employees. This model makes it hard for leaders to believe that their employees can be motivated by higher purpose to do things that are not contractually rewarded. However, for leaders to take higher purpose seriously, they must imagine an unimaginable organization of excellence in which people are purpose-driven, sacrifice for the common good, and collaborate beyond expectations. The first counterintuitive step in creating a purpose-driven organization is thus to drop the assumption that employees cannot be inspired by higher purpose and to envision a purpose-driven organization.

Getting Started: Tools and Exercises

To envision a purpose-driven organization, try the exercise described in this chapter. Identify some key people from different parts of your organization, and ask them to engage with you in the following way:

First make a list of words or phrases that describe the organization at its best. Then examine the following checklist. Identify other words and phrases that capture aspects of your aspiration. When you are done, write a paragraph that describes what you believe is possible. Share and integrate your visions. In doing this, you help your people envision the purpose-driven organization.

Checklist: The Positive, Purpose-Driven Organization

MEANINGFUL INTENT
☐ We have a higher purpose.
☐ We have a shared vision.
☐ We are driven by a strategic plan.
☐ We are pursuing possibilities we believe in.

POSITIVE PEER PRESSURE
☐ We see more positive norms emerge.
☐ Our expectations align with the purpose.
☐ Negative peer pressure becomes positive.
☐ Peers confront the underperformers.

SPONTANEOUS CONTRIBUTION
☐ We surrender our self-interest.
☐ We sacrifice for the common good.
☐ We spontaneously give of ourselves.
☐ Our ego goals become contribution goals.

COLLABORATIVE RELATIONSHIPS
☐ We have a win-win mentality.
☐ Our competition becomes collaboration.
☐ Our teamwork is natural.
☐ We become a dynamic whole.

FULL ENGAGEMENT
☐ We care about what we are doing.
☐ We are engaged in our purpose.
☐ We are giving all we have.
☐ We are fully committed to our purpose.

CREATIVE EFFORT
☐ We try new ideas.
☐ We take intelligent risks.
☐ We improvise.
☐ We make discoveries as we move forward.

FULL INCLUSION
☐ We make the outliers feel invited in.
☐ We see the obstinate people beginning to believe.
☐ We all feel like we belong.
☐ We lose no energy dealing with resisters.

POSITIVE REGARD
☐ We use affirming language.
☐ We do not judge anyone.
☐ We express positive appreciation.
☐ We value one another.

(continued)

SHARED VULNERABILITY

☐ We share personal vulnerability.

☐ We reveal our own mistakes.

☐ We ask questions when we fail to understand.

☐ We ask one another for help.

CONSTRUCTIVE CONFRONTATION

☐ We see truth as more important than power.

☐ We communicate in an authentic way.

☐ We share what we really feel.

☐ We respectfully challenge ideas.

SPONTANEOUS LEADERSHIP

☐ Our leadership emerges spontaneously.

☐ Our leadership moves from person to person.

☐ Each of us leads as appropriate.

☐ Each of us initiates as needed.

COLLECTIVE LEARNING

☐ We co-create learning.

☐ We piggyback on to one another's contributions.

☐ We create a shared mind-set.

☐ We feel we can figure out anything.

TIME DISCIPLINE

☐ We maintain a quick pace.

☐ We keep to our planned schedules.

☐ We deliver results on a timely basis.

☐ We persist as needed to meet deadlines.

RECOGNIZABLE SUCCESS

☐ We experience recognizable success.

☐ We receive praise from those we serve.

☐ We attract new business.

☐ Outsiders want to work with us.

JOYFUL ACHIEVEMENT

☐ We take joy in our outcomes.

☐ We infect one another with positive energy.

☐ Our growth creates enthusiasm.

☐ We love the work.

ATTRACTION OF RESOURCES

☐ Our success breeds success.

☐ New people want to work for us.

☐ New customers flow to us.

☐ Our work is in high demand

CHAPTER EIGHT

STEP 2 Discover the Purpose

In the introduction to *Timeless Wisdom: Passages for Meditation from the World's Saints and Sages,* by Eknath Easwaran, the author begins with a parable. It is a story about an ancient sculptor in India who carves elephants from stone. One day a king visits and asks the man for the secret of his great artistry.

The sculptor explains that once a large stone is secured, he spends a very long time studying the stone. He does this with complete concentration and will not allow himself to be distracted. At first he sees nothing but the huge rock. Then, over a long period he begins to notice something in the substance of the great stone. His expanding awareness begins with a feeling and turns into a vague impression, a scarcely discernable outline.

As he continues to ponder with an open eye and an eager heart, the outline intensifies, until the moment when the sculptor sees the elephant inside the rock. At this moment he sees what no other human can see, and only he has the capacity to bring the elephant out of the rock.

Only when he sees the outline does the sculptor begin the chiseling. In doing so, he is always obedient to the revealed outline. In the process, he connects with the elephant inside the stone. The experience is emotional and tends to defy conventional logic. He feels the future. He feels called to nurture it into being. With this emotional awareness, the sculptor gains an even more intense singleness of purpose. He chips away every bit of rock that is not the elephant. What remains is the elephant.[49]

Michelangelo said something similar: "I saw the angel in the marble and carved until I set him free."

Staring at Rocks

We know a person who was asked to lead an organization. He had a six-month lead time, and during those six months he spent every spare moment staring at his rock, the organization he was about to lead.

As he did, he recorded ideas regarding one topic: his vision for the organization. He wrote hundreds of pages, knowing the final product had to be less than a sentence. The process continued through the six months and then three weeks into the new job. Finally, he stated the initial vision and purpose. He captured it in four words, but over the next six months, he made small refinements. For the next two and a half years, he carved away anything that was not elephant. He now reflects on his accomplishments with a sense of awe.

A leader can make the unusual choice to sit and concentrate on the rock that is their life or the organization that they seek to lead. At first they may see nothing. If they continue, they may notice vague impressions that turn into a barely discernible outline of possibilities. As these intensify, they may begin to see an elephant to be carved. It is likely to be a vision no one else can see.

From the vision, the leader may find the courage to chisel. If they stay within the outline, they may, like a mother with life in her womb, become emotionally attached to a latent relationship or latent organization that has the potential to exist in the world. As this connection strengthens, their singleness of purpose may further intensify. With all their might, mind, heart, and strength, they may labor to give birth to a new version of self or a new version of their organization.

Discovering your organization's higher purpose is a lot like staring at a rock and seeing the elephant in it. It is not easy, but done well, it connects the people in the organization to the reason why the organization does what it does. It converts agents into principals. It reduces moral hazard in the principal–agent model. It emancipates the creative and collaborative energy of the organization.

Conventional Work

The work that brings an elephant from a rock is not conventional. At a global oil company, we met with members of a task force who had been charged by the CEO with defining the purpose of the organization. They handed us a document that articulated a purpose, a mission, and a set of values, a document that represented months of work. We told them candidly that their document had no power—their analysis and debate had produced only politically acceptable platitudes. They reacted with anger.

The members of the task force had been operating from the conventional mind-set. They assumed that creating a collective purpose statement could emerge from conventional, politically grounded, conversations. They had operated from self-interest and conflict avoidance. They used only their heads to invent a higher purpose.

You do not invent higher purpose. It already exists. It lurks in the great organizational rock known as the workforce. It comes forward only when you care enough to reflect on the human system. You can discover it by scaling empathy, by feeling the deepest needs of the collective. This involves asking provocative questions, and listening and reflecting.

In the movie *Gandhi* when Gandhi leaves South Africa and arrives in India, his mentor suggests that he will eventually lead India. Gandhi responds, "I do not know India."

The mentor says, "Then go find India."

Gandhi buys a third-class train ticket and spends extensive time with the impoverished people of India. With the objective of better understanding their suffering, he inquires, observes, feels, and reflects. As he does this, Gandhi begins to see the elephant that is India.

Shortly after returning from his extended trip, Gandhi attends a political meeting. In his speech, he first challenges the conventional, self-interested assumptions of the Indian leaders. His shocking challenge captures the attention of the audience. Then Gandhi simply states what India is about: "bread and salt." He continues to speak with power about the condition of the people and what real leaders must do if the country is to prosper. The audience is overwhelmed and transformed by his understanding and authenticity. Decades later, the image of "bread and salt"—having ownership of and control over your own resources—would be used to inspire the people to finally overthrow the British rule.

Unlike the executives at the oil company, Gandhi behaved like the sculptor who examines a rock. He went to the people, and he reflected deeply. In doing so, he was practicing generalized empathy, which allowed him to give voice to the soul of India. He was able to articulate an authentic higher purpose. He did not invent it. He discovered it and gave it voice.

Finding Purpose in a University

We interviewed Deborah Ball, former dean of the School of Education at the University of Michigan, who provides another example of finding an organization's purpose. Like most companies, professional schools experience mission drift. While an organization may have a purpose, that purpose is often lost or displaced, and the goal that emerges is to be in service of the needs to the power elites who run the organization. As a new dean, Ball wanted to clarify her organization's purpose so she could "enable collective action."

To "learn and unlearn the organization," as she put it, she interviewed every faculty member. She expected to find much diversity of opinion—and she did. But she also found surprising commonality, what she called "an emerging story" about the faculty's strong desire to have a positive impact on society. The word *emerging* is important. By listening, she was bringing a new meaning system into existence. Ball wrote up what she learned and shared it with the people she interviewed. She listened to their reactions and continued to refine their story.

This was not just a listening tour. It was an extended, disciplined, iterative process of organizational learning. Ball said, "You identify gold nuggets, work with them, clarify them, integrate them, and continually feed them back." She referred to the process as "collective creation."

As that work continued, she became convinced that the school had particular strengths to bring about social good. For example, it had the capacity to influence how other institutions around the world trained teachers, it addressed issues of educational affordability, and it served underrepresented populations. Ball concluded that these focal points had the greatest potential to integrate faculty members' efforts, draw impressive new hires, and attract funding for research, so she highlighted them as crucial elements of the school's collective identity.

A Purpose Finder: Helping Others Find Purpose

We also interviewed Nick Craig, an executive coach who has spent the last decade helping thousands of people find their purpose. His work transforms lives, and Nick loves doing it. He joyfully told us story after story.

Interestingly, Nick began with an account of personal transformation. He told us of his childhood, and described a period of despair and desperation. One day, as a preteen, he was standing in a bookstore when it suddenly became clear that he had to make a decision: "I could continue to live in the victim mentality or I could live in a mentality of possibility. I began to take accountability for my life. Others chose to remain in the victim mentality, and we have ended up in very different places."

Waking Up to Personal Purpose

"My life mission is to wake you up and have you finally be home," Nick said. He believes that when people articulate their purpose, they find their most authentic self. They feel like they have finally found home. He is always helping people look for words that help them articulate the greatness that is already inside them.

Nick has written a book called *Leading from Purpose*.[50] We interviewed him in the middle of his writing, and he could hardly express all the things he was feeling. He told us that individual purpose is already wired in. "If we do not find our purpose, we cannot lead from it. When we find it, we awake, we become conscious and aware. In gaining this awareness, we transform. With a new perspective, we gain a sense of meaning. We take accountability. We feel empowered, and we gain an increased desire to create and contribute."

"Purpose leads to action," Nick said. Once we find our own purpose, we gain clarity of focus and we gain the confidence to move forward into uncertainty. The journey through uncertainty ensures deep learning. As we travel, purpose gives the energy and enthusiasm we need to deal with adversity we inevitably encounter. We become more resilient and we learn things others cannot learn.

He says that "when we step into our purpose, our roles no longer define us. As we become centered in our purpose, we become internally directed, our power comes from within. We become willing to do hard things." Nick continually repeated the sentence "When you have purpose, you choose to do the hard, right thing, rather than the easy, wrong thing."

Nick told us that when we live in our purpose, we create "good stress." Instead of living in the threat response, we live in the challenge response. "In the challenge response, we move forward learning and growing as we seek to create. As we do, we take on a paradoxical quality. Purpose gives us the strength to continue in uncertainty, and it gives us vulnerability that comes with doing so. When we are both strong and vulnerable, we find and present our authentic self."

The Power of Personal Purpose

To help people find their purpose, Nick says he helps them examine their "magical moments in childhood," their "crucible stories," and their "life passions." As people share these, Nick listens deeply and helps them look for the threads.

The moment someone finds their purpose, they pulse with excitement. They create a purpose statement that carries power. When they share it, everyone else lights up. "As they listen to the words, everyone in the room gets a tingling in their body," Nick says. "The test is this question: 'Does the curious little boy or girl in you suddenly show up; if not, you have not found your purpose.'"

About purpose, discipline, and growth, Nick observed,

I have studied every religion. I have a network of friends filled with people who are spiritually disciplined or military folks who are members of the Special Forces. I think spiritual discipline and military discipline produce people of higher purpose. Because they are pursuing something bigger than self, they are willing to do the hard, right thing rather than the easy, wrong thing. Purpose exposes your integrity gaps. It lets you know the score. Purpose does not let you take a vacation. It will not let you go. It pulls you into the next crucible. Eventually, you begin to see the next crucible as a gift.

Personal Purpose to Organizational Purpose

About organizational purpose, Nick told us, "Personal purpose is a litmus test for organizational purpose." His point is that when we find our personal purpose, it transforms us. When the organizational purpose is articulated, it has the same transformational power. When people feel it at the personal level, they can begin to envision feeling something similar at the collective level. They know that the organizational purpose is something more than a set of PR words. Today, many organizations employ a marketing or a communications firm to come up with the company's purpose. It is possible that they succeed, but it is not likely or probable. "People have to live in personal purpose in order to find collective purpose," Nick says. "Madison Avenue is not likely to get you there."

Finding your organizational purpose is transformational. You gain the potential to make a unique shift that is not being made by competitors. Prior to having a purpose, you cannot see the shift. Even if you could, you would have no appetite for the shift.

The Purpose Workshop

People who are clear about their personal purpose are more able to turn conventional conversations into authentic dialogues. Nick often conducts a three-day workshop that consists of a cluster of genuine dialogues. In the first day and a half, he aims to bring everyone to their personal purpose. It is grueling work, but the people find it profoundly powerful.

He then spends a day and a half helping them discover the organizational purpose. As the workshop unfolds, Nick creates partners and puts them into groups of four. He asks each group to imagine the collective purpose and to write a story about how that purpose might be manifested in three years. The two partners choose what they most value and then share that in the foursome. The four evaluate what they have shared. The process is repeated in a group of eight. In this complex undertaking, something unpredictable happens predictably. At some point, someone articulates a narrative so compelling that everyone recognizes the power.

While the words in the narrative are important, they are not what matters most. What matters is the room, the sacred space, the authentic dialogue that emerges. In that dialogue, learning goes to an unconventional level. People begin to share and discover new things. The purpose begins to come out of the shadows.

Nick described the process:

> I have a set of steps that I take them through, but I have to pay close attention and know when to stop following my own formula. When the magic shows up, I have to adapt and do what is necessary to keep the magic going. It is not easy because the process is not sustainable. Everything colludes to bring it down. I have to work hard to keep it flowing. I have to be in a higher state of influence. I have to be authentic, and I have to keep them authentic. I try to help them understand that the precious words they are producing are not as important as the collective, behavioral state in which they are producing them. I have to invite them to stay in this higher level of collective learning.

Nick likened this elevated state to something from our own work. We call it "the fundamental state of leadership."[51] The concept, based on science, suggests that both individuals and groups can consciously choose to increase their sense of purpose, integrity, empathy, and humility. In this state, relationships change, and interactions give rise to new resources.

Discovering the Organizational Purpose

Nick provided some specific organizational examples. One of the most striking was the Development Bank of Singapore. Nick worked with the bank's top management team, helping executives find their individual purpose and then turn their attention to the collective purpose. He did not want them to invent their purpose; he wanted them to discover it.

Nick had the executives begin with childhood stories. Some of them spoke of visiting the bank as children, such as one woman who told of taking her piggy bank to her aunt who was a teller in the bank. Another executive spoke of customer appreciation letters that contained the word *joy*. Eventually, someone suggested that banking and joy were related. This suggestion brought a strong rebuke from the group. Over the next day, however, the word *joy* kept coming up.

Eventually, a purpose statement emerged: "Making banking joyful." Nick tested the validity by asking for stories that illustrated the statement. The executives shared many stories. The team began to realize that they were reconnecting to something that had once been a central aspect of the bank. In making the statement, they were articulating a purpose that had once led the bank.

The notion that many on the team had earlier so strongly rejected now became a source of energy. Having articulated their personal purposes and their collective purpose, the team moved forward with a new vision. As they began to live it, signs could be seen by people at lower levels that an authentic change was occurring. The executive team dedicated funding to examining customer interactions and joy. They initiated 75 change projects related to joy. They redesigned the top floor of the bank to encourage and work on joyfulness. They reshaped marketing to accentuate the theme. They increased investments in customer-focused solutions and apps.

The bank was transformed. Evidence of the transformation can be seen in a single conversation. In Singapore at Chinese New Year, it is a tradition to trade one's old money for new money. This means long lines at banks. Driven by the notion of "joyful banking," a lower-level employee decided to put out portable ATMs.

The portable ATMs were a big success. On a TV show, the CEO was complimented for his foresight. He accepted the compliment even though he had no idea that the portable ATM program had been initiated. After the show, he called his CIO and asked about the ATMs and why he had not been informed. The CIO responded, "Well, if we are going to make banking joyful, we need to get you out of being involved in every decision."[52]

Think about the last sentence. What does it is say about the shift from the conventional to the inclusive perspective? What does it say about the emergence of a new culture, a culture of excellence?

While this example may suggest that discovering an authentic higher purpose is easy and fun, in reality it is not. It is often quite difficult to convince leaders of the power of higher purpose. Sometimes leaders come up with a purpose not because it's an authentic purpose but because an important investor or director suggested it or because they think they can fix a problem by motivating employees. So they come up with a purpose that will look good as a PR statement. Examples like that of the Singapore bank do not impress them because the purpose statements do not fit their preconceived notion of what good PR looks like. So they miss out on opportunities to organically discover their authentic purpose.

For example, we spoke to a midlevel professional whose boss had directed her to lead a project to develop a purpose statement for the organization. She had begun working on the project and found the task daunting. We shared examples of purpose statements from other organizations, and she grew excited. In the next meeting with her boss, she shared an example that she felt was particularly relevant. He rejected the example. The statement reflected a level of authenticity and commitment that would require change. This fell outside his expectations He had expected an easy solution, some good PR words. He had no interest in doing the work of discovering an authentic purpose and aligning with it.

Waking Up the Many

Not all of Nick's cases have had outcomes as impressive as that of the Development Bank of Singapore. Nick said,

I have become a realist. The people who write business books make it look like their particular tool always works. Nothing always works. Organizations are at different levels of change readiness. When they tell me they already have a purpose statement, I cringe, but I do not challenge them. I accept where they are, and I begin working with them. Often when they find their individual purposes, they begin to see that their organizational purpose is not real.

I often ask them, "If your organization disappeared tomorrow, how long would it take for others to replace what you were doing? How is your collective contribution unique? What are you doing that no one else is doing?"

They sometimes realize there is something the organization is meant to do differently. There is an underlying ethos that needs to be tapped. Previously they failed to see this; they thought they were in the business of coming up with words. They begin to see it is not about the words; it is about profound power. If they can work harder and find their real purpose, they can pop the entire organization to a higher level.

Nick told us that some people get this, so they begin to lead. They wake up others, who will wake up the many. When that happens, people's lives are never the same, and the organization is never the same. Work becomes more sacred. Boredom disappears. Everyone has energy. You no longer have to police the people. Leadership becomes easy. You almost feel like you are somehow cheating. The people are doing what they are supposed to be doing without your trying to control them. Nick was describing the transformation of the principal–agent problem.

Nick closed our conversation with a provocative thought: "Purpose is not necessarily happiness. Purpose is about intention and action, not happiness. It often produces happiness, but in the middle of the journey, it can be very taxing."

Nick said that purpose has implications for leadership. People who have a genuine purpose see the potential in others, and they seek to link the others to the collective higher purpose. In every interaction, they are linking the people to a higher image. As we would put it, they are all seeing the same "elephant," and magic happens. The need for control declines because the people begin to lead themselves. The organization begins to learn and grow.

Summary

In the principal–agent model, people view the principal or CEO as the "leader" if they visualize a hierarchical relationship with the leader at the top. They assume that the task of a leader is to know and announce the purpose of the organization. Higher purpose is not invented by the CEO, it is collectively discovered. Finding higher purpose requires disciplined reflection, authentic dialogue, and hearing the emerging story of the organization. The scaling up of empathy means recognizing the suffering and the joys of the whole.

When the organization discovers and articulates a higher purpose, that higher purpose provides meaning, gives rise to moral action, repels some and attracts others, gives rise to new practices, transforms peer pressure, gives rise to collaboration, drives renewal, and gives the organization access to previously latent resources. The second counterintuitive step in creating a purpose-driven organization is to discover the higher purpose.

Getting Started: Tools and Exercises

Phase 1. With your working group, watch the scene from *Gandhi* in which Gandhi is told to "go to find India." He takes a train trip and returns to give a speech about bread and salt, a speech that has great impact. Discuss the learning process that gave rise to the insights about bread and salt, and discuss why people began to listen. Review the descriptions in this chapter, and discuss how your working group can go about the process of finding the India in your organization. Agree on the key steps you need to take to discover the purpose of your organization.

Phase 2. Have your working group go out and do interviews with members of the organization and customers/clients. They can ask them these questions:

> ➤ If our organization disappeared tomorrow, how long would it take for another organization to do what we are doing?
>
> ➤ How is our collective contribution unique? What are we doing that no one else is doing?
>
> ➤ What contribution could we make that would increase your loyalty to this organization?

Phase 3. In the working group, have people share their key insights from the interviews. Then review this chapter and formulate a strategy for discovering the purpose of the organization.

CHAPTER NINE

STEP 3 Meet the Need
 for Authenticity

We were on the panel at an academic meeting on the topic of authenticity. We talked about how authentic people have integrity in that they live in accordance with an ideal or higher purpose. They become servants of the purpose or aspiration, which causes them to be internally directed, and they take ownership. Their behavior moves from an ego base to a moral base, and they become better versions of themselves. They pursue the purpose, and in doing so they step outside of normal role expectations and accomplish unusual things. They speak from both the heart and the head, and others discern their authenticity and vulnerability, leading to trust and the emergence of collaborative relationships.

Conventional Assumptions

We opened the discussion to the audience. Most of the professors in the audience were there because they were interested in authenticity research, but they didn't seem to understand it in the way we had just discussed it. Their questions reflected assumptions of transaction and exchange, they could not seem to imagine authenticity.

Making the conventional assumptions about authenticity, they believed that it meant correspondence to the facts. It meant being honest and telling the factual truth. The notion of having a higher ideal and being internally directed and speaking simultaneously from the heart and head seemed outside their conventional perspective. These scholars had learned from cultural experiences, as we all do, to expect people to be externally driven, self-interested, political actors. They expected communication to be distorted by self-interest. They did not expect people to say what they felt and feel what they said.

Authenticity has two dimensions. One dimension is the conventional notion of factual honesty. The second dimension is emotional honesty. Authentic people have both, so they speak from both the head and the heart. Their feelings and their words are congruent. They are not trying to meet role expectations or adjust to a changing political context. They convey a message that reflects a deeply held internal perspective. They are authoring their own unique message.

Assumed Hypocrisy

The skeptical perspective that people are only self-interested political actors permeates managerial practice. For example, one CEO actually told his senior leadership team he did not want to do purpose work because he knew they would not live the purpose. He felt that articulating a higher purpose would simply make the organization devolve into an even more political place where people would use purpose as an excuse to engage in more self-serving behavior. By recognizing that organizations are political systems and hypocrisy is inevitable, he was accepting conventional reality.[53]

A member of the team responded, "Why don't we change that? Let's identify a purpose and a set of values, and live them with integrity."

That earnest comment punctured the existing skepticism. It raised the unusual possibility of pursuing an authentic higher purpose. The executive team considered the possibility and decided to take purpose work seriously. That one comment changed the organization.

A Jolt to the Mind-Set

To understand the power of authentic higher purpose, people need an inclusive mind-set that integrates the reality of constraint with the reality of possibility. They often acquire such a mind-set, as we have seen, through an external jolt that alters thinking.

We interviewed a CFO who had just lived through the fiscal transformation of a troubled organization. He told us he had worked hard to solve the financial problems his organization faced, yet he had made only a minimal impact.

Subsequently, his boss clarified and rearticulated the purpose of the organization and transformed the culture of the organization. In the new culture, people had more control, and trust increased. They became more positive. They had conversations that were more authentic. They collaborated more. People began to go the extra mile for the good of the organization. They agreed to return rather than expend allocated annual budgets. The organization changed, and soon the financial crisis became known as the "financial miracle."

The CFO spoke of the "financial miracle" as a life-changing event. He told us that it had never previously crossed his mind that inspiration, authenticity, trust, and collaboration could solve a major financial problem. He had always assumed that a workforce consisted of self-interested "agents," and the notion of leading an organization in which people willingly sacrificed for the collective good was not imaginable.

The CFO had experienced an epiphany. He now tells his peers in the same industry about the power of authentic purpose and positive culture. He told us, "They do not listen. They say, 'It might have worked in your place, but we are different. It would never work with us. No one is going to willingly give back their unspent budget.'"

The CFO gained a more complex level of understanding that leads him to believe and see possibilities his colleagues do not see.

We should note that his colleagues' defensiveness is due to more than just their experience-based assumptions. CFOs are expected to be experts in finance and shareholder value creation. If this particular CFO's message is true, it means the other CFOs have to acknowledge and explore paths to value creation that are outside of their formal training and the "best practices" of their discipline. This is hard to do. We all share this tendency. Our functional expertise can blind us to paths that lie outside of our discipline boundaries. And even if these paths are pointed out to us, our propensity is to resist them because they do not fit our worldview of what works.

Purpose and Authentic Communication

Conventional culture trains you to present a politically acceptable self. People see that, and it causes them to be indifferent to the messages you communicate because the political correctness diminishes the information value of the messages. As leaders turn to higher purpose, we have observed a trend. They begin communicating in a new and more influential way.

We attended the annual leadership meeting of DTE Energy. Over eight years the company had become increasingly purpose driven. At the meeting, we could see a new pattern that we often observe as a company turns to purpose. Many of the senior people begin to become more intimate, vulnerable, and authentic.

At DTE the annual meeting had always been scripted from start to finish. On the first day, after a presentation on purpose, the CEO, Gerry Anderson, stood up and went off the script. He told a personal story and then spoke about the importance of families. The openness was unexpected but deeply appreciated by the audience.

On the final day, he again spoke from his most intimate experience. He told of John, his uncle and a man of extraordinary worldly accomplishments and renown. John had suffered a heart attack and was dying. Gerry said he went to visit John and began by asking him what he had been thinking about lately. John replied that he had been thinking about all the people in his life. He told a story about his sons, who had recently visited. During the visit, the two sons hugged each other. John said, "It was beautiful."

In the entire conversation, John talked about relationships and never mentioned any of his great achievements or the rewards they brought. Gerry was moved. He said, "For me, it was a message from the future. What really matters, what bring us our greatest meaning, is our relationships."

Gerry began to speak about the difference between leading a *successful life* versus leading a *significant life*. Success tends to be about personal achievement. Significance tends to be about contributing to the good of others. He spoke of the cumulative effect of making many small contributions to the people around us. Then he said, "Investing in relationships does not come to me naturally, so I have decided to work at it." It was clear that everyone was captivated by this revelation. The CEO was confessing a weakness, and people were impressed. People are hungry to hear authentic messages, and the expression of vulnerability is the door to trust.

Gerry told another personal story. He spoke of a lower-level employee who was retiring after 40 years. The person who brought him the news asked Gerry if he might be able to drop into the retirement party for a few minutes. When Gerry checked his calendar, he found that the party was the day of the board meeting. Since he would be having lunch with the board, he declined the invitation.

The experience nevertheless stayed in his mind. He kept thinking about how much his presence might mean to the employee. He began to think that leaving the board meeting for a few minutes would not be a big deal. So he decided to make the visit.

When he walked into the retirement celebration, the person who had made the invitation simply "lit up," and the retiring employee was "dumbfounded" that the CEO was attending his retirement party. Everyone was delighted. The gesture also had an impact on the CEO. He said he also felt "lit up," and he returned to the board meeting filled with positive energy.

The experience, though small, was so positive that Gerry began to ask himself: how could he more regularly make such small but positive investments? So he asked the people who surrounded him to look for and notify him of such opportunities. He closed his story by asking everyone to imagine a company where all 150 top leaders regularly made similar small but positive investments.

At the conclusion of the meeting, we chatted with one of the participants and asked her to assess her experience of the three-day event. She said, "This is so different. Of all of the annual meetings I have attended, this is the best by far. I am so looking forward to what happens to this company."

Why is it that when a company begins to orient to higher purpose, senior people begin to become more intimate, vulnerable, and authentic? One reason is that as senior people try to explain personal and organizational purpose, they find it necessary to illustrate being driven by personal values and purpose. They explain their personal identities and destinies by sharing the experiences from which they stem. They speak of the link between their personal purpose and the organizational purpose by sharing meaningful personal experiences.

While conventional culture trains us to avoid appearing to be vulnerable—seeing it as a sign of weakness—the positive lens calls us to authenticity and vulnerability. In a purpose-driven, positive organization, people have high-quality relationships because it is safe to communicate who they really are.

Authenticity on Wall Street

When we introduce authentic purpose, critics often suggest that it is a naive approach. They tell us, "It would never work on Wall Street."

One CEO whom we interviewed was Jimmy Dunne of Sandler, O'Neil and Partners, a midsize investment bank in New York City.

One day in 2001, Jimmy was playing golf. As he walked off the course, he was given an incomprehensible message. One third of his employees, including two of the three most senior leaders in the organization, had died. The date was September 11, 2001.

From that moment, Jimmy faced severe challenges. He simultaneously mourned the death of his workforce while also trying to save a firm with few remaining resources. In the midst of this intense pressure, Jimmy resolved that he or another senior person would attend every possible funeral of employees who had died on 9/11. This meant Jimmy attended many funerals. In the late hours of each night, he tried to work on the business, that is, to save his company. Today, Jimmy claims that in crisis you discover your deepest values and clarify your highest purpose. He says, "Crisis does not create character. It reveals it."

As Jimmy attended the funerals, one of the first issues he faced was what to do about the salaries and benefits of those who had died. In most organizations, if an employee dies, wages and benefits expire too, perhaps not right away but in a matter of months. Jimmy said: "We had decided early on we were willing to go against the trend. We're willing to do what we thought others were not willing to do."

So what did Jimmy do? The Wall Street investor decided to pay the families of all the dead employees their salaries and bonuses through the end of the year. They would all receive what the dead partner earned in their very best year.

Jimmy went further in clarifying his values and purpose. He asked his CFO if they could repeat the exercise for all of 2002. She said the firm could survive but that doing this would be inconsistent with their fiduciary responsibility to the surviving partners. So Jimmy informed the partners and made the offer that any partner who objected to the practice would be given the opportunity to cash out their ownership share at par. No one objected.

Eventually, the company paid the salaries and benefits for *three* years. Jimmy said that he realized that in doing this, he was jeopardizing the financial viability of the firm, but he was committed to getting the partners' capital back to their families. He says he believes, "It was what Herman Sandler [the founder] would have done," and he was not worried about "conforming to the norm or managing to mediocrity."

Jimmy's last sentence is important because we all conform to norms. In the conventional social setting, our conformity actually draws us toward mediocrity. In organizations it is natural for people to go through the motions. But when people clarify their own deepest values and purpose, their identity and destiny, they, like Jimmy Dunne, become more internally directed. Jimmy told us he was not worried about what was normal but about doing what was right. It was his growing commitment to moral excellence that led him to the "unheard of scenario."

Consequences

Like other companies we have seen, the higher purpose of Sandler was not only to serve the customer in the best way possible but also to have a committed, energized, and trusting workforce that was treated like family. With this in mind, we asked Jimmy how his unusual actions were received.

Jimmy told of widows who gathered in postcrisis therapy sessions. One widow said that many of the widows in her group were from other companies and were financially stretched. Then the story of the Sandler wives came out. The group expressed profound admiration for the values of the firm. Jimmy says that as he listened to the story, he discovered "what brand is," and what it means to have the "Sandler way." In other words, Jimmy was discovering the power of authentic purpose and collaborative culture. Having an authentic purpose and culture differentiates a firm and makes it attractive to those who deal with it.

Both inside and outside the company Sandler was seen as different. Jimmy says, "Our status increased." Inside, the people became increasingly loyal. Outside, support began to flow to the firm, and other companies began to follow the practices of Sandler. In the next few years, the company prospered financially and grew.

Purpose and Practices

Jimmy has become very conscious of the role of authentic purpose and positive culture in the organization. He says the CEO has to set an example of the purpose. He told of a conversation that occurred just before we arrived. A new employee made a mistake that cost the firm a substantial amount of money. Jimmy called him in, and in a respectful way he explored what happened and helped the person derive learning. He then sent the (relieved) employee on his way.

Jimmy asked, "Do you think that is what I wanted to do? No. I wanted to chew him out."

Jimmy explained that he does not have the luxury of following his natural instincts. Every act he take seeps into the culture and creates expectations. He had to treat the employee well because the firm has purpose and values and Jimmy has to live them. If he does not live them, the purpose and values are seen as hypocritical, and everyone becomes cynical.

In the hiring process, Sandler looks for people who are authentic. In describing the process, Jimmy provides a graphic image of who they do *not* hire: "The reason we've got all these people here is because of the painstaking effort we make to try and find the right people, and it is our unwillingness to accept any assholes. They can't survive here."

Jimmy was referring to an ego-driven person. At Sandler, they look for and seek to retain people who are committed to the common good. Jimmy said, "People who are selfish or takers don't last with us." Sandler's higher purpose has led to a culture that values the common good and gives rise to authentic relationships.

Speaking of authentic communication, Jimmy has a rule: you can't talk about someone critically unless that person is in the room. Jimmy explained that once an executive (let's call him John) came to his office to complain about another executive (let's call him Andrew). As John began to talk, Jimmy started dialing a number on his phone, and John asked him who he was calling. "Andrew, of course," said Jimmy. John was shocked—why would you call him?

Jimmy explained that he wanted Andrew to hear what John had to say about him so he could present his side of the story. John expressed his befuddlement: "I came to talk to you in confidence, Jimmy."

Jimmy said, "Oh, I see. So you only want to say these things about Andrew if he cannot hear them?"

Jimmy explained to us that this rule has a profound effect. The company has to deal with very little backstabbing. When there is a conflict, people simply ask themselves: "What would Jimmy say if we took this to him?" In most cases, the matter does not actually come to Jimmy. People sort it out among themselves. The culture is one of openness, authenticity, and trust. It does not need to be micromanaged from the top.

At the end of the interview, Jimmy's assistant whispered something in his ear. Jimmy turned to us and said, "Oh, yes! We actually paid salaries and benefits [for the deceased employees] for 10 years. But I don't talk about the last 7 because we could afford to do it then. It is easy to be generous when you can afford it."

People at the firm know that the purpose of the firm is authentic because it drives the decisions and behaviors of the CEO. The CEO is able to stay away from normal pressures of convenience and follow purpose to patterns of excellence. The firm does unusual things, like paying the families of dead employees, and it reaps unusual rewards in that its culture attracts resources that other, similar firms do not attract. Jimmy Dunne's discovery and enactment of higher purpose was fully authentic.

Summary

In the standard principal–agent model, people are expected to pursue their self-interest. Communication is expected to preserve that self-interest and thus is interpreted as doing that. Contractual mechanisms are deployed to ensure the only dimension of authenticity the model recognizes—factual correctness. There is no role in the model for the second dimension of authenticity—emotional honesty. However, in reality, communication that has both dimensions of authenticity signals that the communicator is internally driven. To have an authentic higher purpose, leaders must become internally driven representatives of the purpose. They consequently sacrifice to align their behavior to the higher purpose, which induces employees to view the higher purpose as authentic and credible. In so doing, they disrupt the status quo. They connect with their employees and others emotionally and the higher purpose begins to seep into the culture. The third counterintuitive step in creating a purpose-driven organization is to communicate higher purpose with authenticity, to communicate from the soul; to recognize and meet the need for authenticity.

Getting Started: Tools and Exercises

Phase 1. Have your people read the chapter and ask them to pay special attention to the cases of Gerry Anderson and of Jimmy Dunn.

Phase 2. Have them write answers to each of the following questions and then hold an open discussion.

➤ In terms of people and relationships, what is your definition of authenticity?

➤ When have you been impressed with an act of authenticity in your professional experience?

➤ What is your most important takeaway from the stories of Gerry Anderson and Jimmy Dunne?

➢ What strikes you about this statement: "Why don't we change that? Let's identify a purpose and a set of values, and live them with integrity"?

➢ What would be the first steps if we as a group determined to become an organization of authentic, higher purpose?

CHAPTER TEN

STEP 4 Turn the Higher Purpose into a Constant Arbiter

Once when we were conducting a program for executives from across the globe, two of the executives shared a problem with us. They said that their boss, the CEO, had fixed a retirement date in the distant future and that he had checked out and had been behaving in completely self-interested ways. The employees all recognized this. While the two executives did not express it that way, they felt that the principal–agent contract was violated. The CEO was not doing his part, and the employees reacted by withdrawing themselves. They came to work, but they did not bring their hearts. They worked only as hard as they were forced to work. The consequences were serious—an organization in decline.

This is what happens in organizations that lack a higher purpose. Everyone becomes vulnerable to the consequences of self-interest. Normally it is not the CEO but midlevel managers and first-line employees who withdraw to conserve their energy and effort. When they withdraw, the organization takes the consequences. Others also become self-interested, and they do not bring their discretionary energy to their tasks. A key to transforming a social system in decay is for someone in some position to discover a higher purpose, articulate it with authenticity, and do so with a constancy that shapes the culture and inspires action.

Conventional Assumptions

Constancy of purpose complements the notion of authenticity. We make it a separate step because it is so important. Yet constancy is difficult to even imagine. The reason is that conventional managers are focused on task completion, so they find it hard to swallow that embracing higher purpose is the start of a never-ending journey rather than arrival at a destination. When we spoke with the CEO of a global professional services company about how to build a purpose-driven organization, his first question was "When will I be done building it?"

His question reflects an assumption that is central to modern organizational culture. In a professional world, time is at a premium. When an employee reaches the managerial ranks, they are already addicted to action. They have a need for achievement that is linked to a checklist mentality. They desire a list of tasks to do, and they determine the quality of their day by how many items are checked off at the end of the day. They yearn for closure.

We responded to the CEO's question by telling a story about another CEO who had been trying for a year to transform his construction company. He showed us his change plan and asked our opinion about it. We told him he deserved an A-minus. He asked, "Why not an A?"

After giving speeches for a year, he thought he was finished—but his people were just beginning to hear his message. He needed to keep clarifying the organization's purpose, and he needed to use the purpose to inspire the people so they would embrace the purpose and make it the arbiter of all decisions. To do this, he needed to be constant, an unwavering symbol of the highest purpose and a regular source of inspiration. He needed to do this until he had a culture inspired and driven by the purpose. When we told him this, he sank back into his chair.

An Unexpected Culture of Inspiration

David Perkins is a four-star general in the US Army. While we were writing this book, he spoke to a packed auditorium at the Center for Positive Organizations. Across the globe, people make common assumptions about the military: It is a hierarchy. It uses authority to obtain the required effort. The audience showed up in large numbers because they were eager to know what a general could possibly say about creating a purpose-driven, positive organization.

General Perkins began by declaring that every type of leadership gets results, including authority figures who are very negative. Toxic leaders and micromanagers, for example, get results. Often this is why they were promoted to their present levels. Their superiors believed, based on their past performance, that they would deliver in the new job. But those senior managers did not pause to investigate how these people achieved results. Leaders who are in the conventional perspective separate ends and means. They emphasize the ends, so they focus less on how the results were achieved.

General Perkins said that it is not surprising that there are so many toxic leaders and micromanagers. Our culture emphasizes grade point averages, standard scores, and merit evaluations, and it teaches that "it is all about you." In organizations, leaders are expected to get results, so it's in the aspiring leader's self-interest to focus on getting results more than on the means by which the results are achieved. In certain settings, particularly in large hierarchies that do repetitive work, toxic leaders and micromanagers are able to drive people and produce the specified outcomes. The problem is that we live in a world of change where even large hierarchies have to deal with new and unforeseen challenges.

Today, every organization, including the military, has to be a learning organization, and such an organization has a need for inspired people who trust their leaders and do the right thing at the right time even when they know that their leader is not watching. In other words, they need people whose motivation is intrinsic, which often derives from embracing an authentic higher purpose that has been communicated with such constancy and clarity by the leaders that it has been internalized by all. Then the people are willing to bring their discretionary energy to work.

Inspiration and Service

General Perkins believes that you inspire people by serving them. When they are in need is when your service matters. He tries to respond immediately to cries for help. He told of being in a battle zone when a member of his senior staff complained because people were not following procedures. They were ignoring him and going directly to Perkins. The staff person implored Perkins to ask people to respect the hierarchy by sending people to him first.

"They are not going to you first because they do not see you as valued added," General Perkins replied. "You are not making a positive difference and serving them. If you were, they would seek you out."

This is an extraordinary account. If you were the direct report of the general, and he said these words to you, what would it tell you about your theory of leadership? How would you respond?

Bullets and Inspiration

General Perkins is serious about nurturing inspirational influence and creating a culture of higher purpose. He is actually engaged in creating a positive, purpose-driven organization. How do we know this?

He told of removing hundreds of senior and midlevel officers who were known for being toxic leaders or for being micromanagers. He described meetings with people at every level and teaching the notion of inspirational leadership. He would even meet with drill sergeants.

In explaining the need for inspirational leadership, he shared stories of people in battle, including people who were badly wounded and completely isolated. These people needed to make their own decisions, which required trust in their leaders, in their peers, and in their mission. They had to have been inspired by their leader before encountering a crisis. He said, "By the time a man has two bullets in him, and he is required to continue to make key decisions, if he has not already been inspired, it is too late."

Attentional Gravity

As we've seen from the people featured in this book, from Shauri to Jimmy Dunne to Nick Craig, a person who embraces a higher purpose is transformed, and part of the transformation is that the person becomes a living symbol. They are the message. Everything they say and do is an authentic representation of what a person with a particular higher purpose would do. Others who watch the person recognize the common good and understand the highest purpose.

General Perkins shared experiences of reuniting with people who had served under him years before. Often, they recalled their most meaningful experiences. They would say things like "I remember what you said and did 20 years ago when we were in trouble."

One man was recently promoted to command a battalion. He wrote and said, "When I was in your unit, I watched everything you did, and I wrote it down. When I got promoted, I went back and read it all. I am going to try to do what I saw you do." This loyalty does not happen unless the leader constantly lives by and models the higher purpose and the people believe it is authentic.

General Perkins said what so many leaders told us: A leader is the center of attentional gravity, and in tough times the focus is on the leader. Constancy matters. "People are keeping book on you. You must represent what right looks like."

Morality

Notice the link between morality and inspiration. General Perkins is saying that leadership is about modeling the courage to do the right thing. When your conscience triumphs over fear, you represent what is right. When you constantly do what is right, even when it is hard to do, you inspire others.

General Perkins, like Jimmy Dunne, said it takes a long time to build a positive culture. But in times of difficulty, you have your most impact. You show who you really are when you are under the greatest stress and everyone is watching. He said, "On our worst days is when we need to be most positive."

The Arbiter of All Decisions

When a higher purpose is authentic and constant, it eventually becomes the driver and arbiter of all decisions, like the purpose of joyful banking at the Development Bank of Singapore. Every act then aligns and the organization transforms. This is hard to imagine.

We were slated to explore the value of purpose and vision one evening after a company dinner. In the hours before dinner, all the managers met in small groups to do the unpleasant work of downsizing. When we went on, we asked how many of the small groups began their difficult work of downsizing by first examining the company's purpose and values. The answer was none. The managers could not imagine why they should do such a thing. They had a real problem to solve, and the need to downsize had nothing to do with purpose or values.

They were right that their problem solving had nothing to do with their purpose and values. In fact, despite the signs on the wall, they did not have a purpose or values. If the words on the wall were authentic, they would have permeated the consciousness of those at the meeting. This consciousness would have altered how they did the downsizing. They would have done what Nick Craig taught us: follow purpose to do the "hard, right things." Hard, right things differentiate an organization from the pack, and they produce unusual, long-term results. Every person who left or stayed would have had an experience demonstrating that the company values people and has an exceptionally positive culture. The commitment of those who stayed would be higher. The value of the company would be greater.

In many organizations, stating a purpose is simply an exercise to meet expectations. It is a game that results in increased hypocrisy, which produces increased workforce cynicism. In stating an inauthentic purpose, the leader does positive harm and lowers the value of the organization. A test of authenticity is constancy. Is the purpose the arbiter of all decisions?

Social Pressure and Inauthenticity

Many organizations state a purpose because of external social pressure. Today, most organizations are expected to have a purpose statement. Even leaders who do not believe in purpose face pressure from board members, investors, employees, and other stakeholders to articulate a higher purpose.

This pressure sometimes leads to statements like the one produced by the task force at the oil company mentioned in chapter 8. When a company announces and displays its purpose and values, but the words do not govern the behavior of senior leadership, the statement rings hollow. Everyone recognizes the hypocrisy, and the workforce becomes more cynical. The process does more harm than good. An authentic purpose is not the outcome of a technique to produce a dazzling PR statement but a genuine reason for being. It is communicated with authenticity and constancy.

Splitting Versus Integrating

One of our associates helps companies discover their highest purpose. A leader he works with said, "We have discovered a financial problem, so we are going to put aside our work on purpose until things get better."

That CEO has categorized his to-do list. One objective on the list is to create a purpose-driven organization. Another is to remain financially viable. Since remaining financially viable is a short-term issue of survival and establishing a higher purpose is not, the former drives out the latter.

While he does not realize it, his logic keeps him in the reactive and conventional mind-set. He logically separates all his problems and works on them individually. He treats purpose as just another task on his to-do list, a nice tool to bring to the organization, but in doing so, he destroys the ability of the organization to discover its purpose.

He cannot see that continually clarifying and communicating the highest purpose *is* the highest purpose of a leader. He does not see the connections between purpose and all else that is done. Simply put, leaders should not split the pursuit of higher purpose from other business decisions. Rather, they should integrate the decision making so purpose is the constant driver.

Constancy of purpose means purpose is the tie breaker when the organization chooses between making higher profit and acting in a manner consistent with the "why" of the organization. It is not a message on the walls that is meant to fool employees. It is the constant integrator of all decisions and guides the solving of all problems.

The Constant Arbiter of All Decisions

Of all the people we interviewed, no one spoke of leadership and constancy of purpose more eloquently than Tony Meola. Tony is the recently retired head of US consumer operations at Bank of America. Tony is a leader who understands the ongoing nature of purpose work. He says that leadership is relentlessly difficult because it involves moving the institution—and existing cultures tend to impede movement. As extensions of the culture, managers end up resisting the change as well. Organizational complexity and competing demands also impede movement.

Tony overcomes these obstacles by treating operational excellence as a destination and allowing no other pressures to distract him from it. He emphasizes operational skills and leadership in employee training and development, and he brings that focus to every conversation, every decision, every problem his team faces. He is always asking, "Will this make us better operators?"

Over time this constancy of purpose wins. Tony says, "When you hold it constant like that, when you never waver, an amazing thing happens. They realize that the purpose is real. The purpose sinks in to the collective consciousness. The culture changes, and the organization begins to perform at a higher level. Processes become simpler and easier to execute and sustain. People start looking for permanent solutions rather than stop-gap measures that create more inefficiencies through process variations."

Tony told us that embracing this position has meant saying no to anything that doesn't reflect it. In the call center, for example, a proposal was made to invest additional resources in technology and people so that the group could answer customers' questions faster and better and handle 25 percent more inquiries. But the project was rejected because when managers and employees asked themselves whether it would make them better operators, the answer was no. That realization forced them to ask how the operations themselves could be changed to eliminate failures that produced call center inquiries in the first place. The focus on higher purpose transformed the thinking and improved the outcome.

When a leader communicates the purpose with constancy, as Tony has done, the purpose becomes the arbiter of all decisions.

Employees internalize the commitment. They begin to believe in the purpose. The change is thus signaled from the top, and it unfolds from the bottom.

Summary

Because of the focus on contractual outcomes in the traditional principal–agent model, organizations do not typically rely on higher purpose as a driver of decisions, so the question of constantly communicating the higher purpose does not arise. However, for an organization to make purpose the arbiter of all decisions, leaders must constantly and clearly communicate the purpose. This constant message reduces reliance on costly, explicit, contractual incentives. The fourth counterintuitive step in creating a purpose-driven organization is thus to turn the higher purpose into a constant message and make the purpose the arbiter of all decisions.

Getting Started: Tools and Exercises

Phase 1. Have everyone read the chapter.

Phase 2. Hold a meeting of your work group to discuss the following questions:

- ➤ In introducing higher purpose, why would a CEO ask, "When will I be done?"
- ➤ What is constancy of purpose?
- ➤ What does it mean to have a purpose that is the arbiter of all decisions?
- ➤ What happens when economic value added is the arbiter of all decisions?
- ➤ What was General Perkins communicating when he eliminated the many toxic managers and micromanagers?

➢ What happens if an executive like Tony Meola responds to every proposal by asking, "How will this make us better operators?"

Phase 3. Have each person consider their current organization and propose a question like the one Tony asked. Have everyone share their question. Attempt to specify an integrated statement that could be the constant arbiter for the entire organization.

CHAPTER ELEVEN

STEP 5 Stimulate Learning

One day, we were in a studio making a presentation, and one of the sound technicians seemed to hang on our every word. After the session, he approached us. He told us that at one time he was a supervisor of a team of technicians in the company, but he had given it up and retired. That day, he was working as an independent contractor. He reflected on the time as a supervisor and said, "I made a lot of mistakes. After all these years, I still remember some of the things I did, and I ask myself, why did I do that?"

He looked away and reflected, then turned back. With some feeling he said, "You know, very few of those issues had anything to do with producing things. They had to do with relationships. I did not understand. I made lots of mistakes. It is hard do the right thing when you do not see the people and the relationships; you only see the job to be done."

That same day, another man who does similar work spoke to us. With deep admiration, he talked of his boss. He said his boss had evolved into a man of wisdom, and everyone in the organization held him in high esteem. This fellow told us about a performance review: His boss indicated that this man's performance was fine, and he needed to keep up what he was doing. Then he said, "Let me be clear. The most important thing is your family. You stay here too long. You need to get your work done, go home, and be with your family."

As he shared this, displaying vulnerability, the man was near tears. He said, "Can you imagine what it means when you hear words like that from your boss? I cannot believe how lucky I am to work for a man like that."

In these stories we can see an important contrast. One man saw only the task to be done. People were simply a means to an end. To this day he regrets what he did as a supervisor. He now recognizes that it is "hard do the right thing when you do not see the people and the relationships; you only see the job to be done."

The other man had a boss who, showing greater cognitive complexity, recognized the need to get the job done and also saw people as having inherent value. It was his responsibility to care for, inspire, challenge, and support his people.

The first man had a conventional view. He was independent and task focused, and his job was to solve problems by conceptualizing and implementing strategies. The second man was interdependent, and he had an inclusive view. He was focused on a task, and he was focused on people. He was about strategy, and he was about culture. He was about getting the job done, and he was about meeting the human needs of his people.

Convention and Inclusion

People tend to be promoted into management according to length of time in the organization, technical expertise, and their track record in producing results. The emphasis on producing results makes people self-serving and tends to put emphasis on task completion.

As General Perkins pointed out, conventional culture values results more than relationships, with little focus on how the results were achieved. This splits results from culture, emphasizing the results and destroying the culture. As the first man said, "It is hard do the right thing when you only see the job to be done."

Purpose and Prosocial Behavior

As we saw in chapter 2, when people embrace a purpose-driven life, they benefit from many scientifically demonstrated health benefits. They are also more likely to take initiative, persist in meaningful tasks, and listen to negative feedback. That is, they are more likely to learn how to be successful.[54]

Yet their success orientation is not selfish. They are also more likely to assist and motivate others, stimulating them to discover new ideas and engage in creative acts. Purpose-driven people are personally growing, and they desire to promote the growth in others. This is called "prosocial motivation."

An Orientation to Growth

Recently, we were picked up by a limo driver named Louis. He immediately engaged us in conversation, often interspersing in it a full-body laugh.

We learned that Louis, a 60-year-old African American, grew up in Tennessee, left school in the eleventh grade and moved to Detroit. His one talent was that he knew how to work hard. He started off making $1,000 a week when many of his neighbors were making $200. Yet they were better off because he squandered his money on alcohol, drugs, and women. He was going nowhere.

Sharing a spiritual conversion story, he said, "I just could not go on living a meaningless life. I began searching for something more, and then I started meeting people and learning things."

Louis loves learning, and he loves helping other people grow and learn. He told of a recent conversation in his car. He picked up an executive who had had a six-hour flight delay and was in a very bad mood. Given his purpose to help others grow, Louis said he had to figure out how to lift the man.

After considerable reflection, Louis asked the man, "Tomorrow are you going to feel better than you feel right now?"

The man nodded and said yes. Louis said, "Why wait until tomorrow?"

The man was shocked. Then he laughed. He said, "You are right. Why wait? You just made me a better person. My family is going to have a better evening tonight because of you."

As Louis finished the story, he launched into another full-body laugh. Then he said, "That is my life. I am here to help people. I never want to stop learning, and I never want to stop helping other people learn."

Louis may or may not recognize it, but he is a transformational leader. The story of Louis the limo driver is the same story we heard from many CEOs of purpose-driven companies. They originally had a conventional perspective, but then they had some personal experience that brought deep change and a sense of purpose and meaning. They began to grow, and their orientation to others changed. Purpose-driven leaders tend to become facilitators of human growth.

An Orientation to Growth

Psychologist Carol Dweck identifies two measurable orientations she calls "the fixed mind-set" and "the growth mind-set." In the fixed mind-set intelligence and talent are an either/or proposition. You have them, or you do not. People with the fixed mind-set tend to be self-oriented in that they strive to look smart, avoid failure, and avoid the embarrassment of exposed incompetence. Their learning is dampened because of the anxiety that comes with a fixation on avoiding mistakes and performing well.

People with the growth mind-set are different. They believe that talent and intelligence can be enhanced through effort. They yearn for learning and seek out challenges. They see failure as an element of learning.

If a manager has a fixed mind-set, Dweck's research shows that the person tends to punish dissent, seek revenge when rejected, reduce effort in the face of setbacks, see employees as incapable of change, convey a willingness to judge, provide little coaching, and ignore improvements made by employees. If a manager has a growth mind-set, the person is open to dissenting opinions, tends to prac-tice forgiveness, persists to win-win solutions, assumes employees can be developed, tends to both challenge and nurture employees, has a zest for teaching, and reinforces observed improvements. A leader with a growth mind-set is focused on and committed to the growth of others.[55]

Louis is an example of a person who shifted from the fixed to the growth mind-set. Many CEOs enter their role carrying the mind-set of the conventional principal–agent model, which assumes that people are effort averse. They believe that people work for money, and if they are not monitored, they will underperform; they will withhold their effort. So it takes money plus control to get people to simply meet expectations. Managers have to work hard just to get people to do what is expected and do not expect them to exceed expectations. Their perspective makes it difficult for them to see how organizational higher purpose can lead employees to give more than their explicit monetary rewards incentivize them to give.

Managers with a higher-purpose perspective accept that work can be unappealing but see that an authentic higher purpose can change how people view their work and lead to an organization in which the workforce is highly engaged and willingly exceeds expectations.

The research on engagement shows that compensation is a con-tributor to engagement, but it is not the most important contributor. The most important contributor is the quality of leadership and the creation of a positive culture.[56] In an organization of high engagement, people have a sense of clarity and control. Leaders provide clear expectations and the necessary technical resources to support what needs to be done. Leaders also recognize and respond to individual needs. They also do one other thing. They attend to the need for meaning, purpose, learning, and development. They connect their people to a meaningful future and help them see opportunities for growth within their current jobs and in future jobs inside and outside the organization. The paradoxical, empirical fact is that leaders who accelerate the learning, growth, and development of their people have the highest retention rates.[57] Their people are learning and growing and willingly contributing to the common good.

Zingerman's

Zingerman's is a company, started in 1982 by Paul Saginaw and Ari Weinzweig, that has a collection of restaurants and food-related organizations in and around Ann Arbor, Michigan. The company is one of the local treasures, legendary for great food and great service. Many consider it one of the top 25 food markets in the world. It is often mentioned as an example of a purpose-driven, positive organization. We interviewed co-owner and cofounder Ari Weinzweig and asked him what the higher purpose of Zingerman's was. He shared the company's mission statement:

> We share the Zingerman's experience
> Selling food that makes you happy
> Giving service that makes you smile
> In passionate pursuit of our mission
> Showing Love and care in all our actions
> To enrich as many lives as we possibly can.

Note that the highest purpose is to show Love, with a capital *L*, and enrich as many lives as possible. Ari told us he wanted to train each of his employees to be a future entrepreneur. He did not expect all the employees to be lifetime employees. Someday they would leave, and when they did, he hoped that they would have developed the capabilities to start their own businesses, even if they were not restaurant-related businesses.

We were intrigued by this unusual commitment to learning and growth. How did Zingerman's integrate its higher purpose into its business operations? Ari said that one of the things the company does consistently is to emphasize the positives and develop in each of its employees a very proactive and growth-oriented outlook on life. Cultivating positivity in employees serves the higher purpose of delighting customers, and the delight of customers loops back to the employees.

Ari spoke of numerous unusual management practices that build trust, promote growth, and facilitate collaboration. For example, the company practices open-book finance: The company opens its books to trainees and teaches them how to run Zingerman's. The employees have to make all the decisions that Ari and other senior executives make routinely—procurement, menu determination, pricing, hiring, and so on. The training program serves two important purposes: First, it teaches employees how to run the business and prepares them to become entrepreneurs. Second, it engenders trust and collaboration.

When asked why he engages in this and so many other unusual practices, Ari answered, "Let me explain to you how many companies are run, and you'll understand why we don't behave like that. Imagine that you have a football team and you have 11 players on offense, each very skilled in playing his position. But while 6 of the players are individually skilled, they don't really understand the larger game. So you might have a wide receiver with great hands and speed but who catches a pass and then hands the ball over to the defensive back—an intentional fumble—because he wants to be a "nice guy" who wants to "share." And you might have 4 players who are individually skilled and know the game but could not care less about the outcome. So you are left with one player—say the quarterback—who is individually skilled, knows the game, and actually cares about winning. Now, no one in his right mind would ever field a football team like that, right? But that's how many companies are run. We don't do that here."

Ari and Paul clearly march to a different drummer. In 2006 Zingerman's produced a vision written from the perspective of the company in 2020. In it we find many statements regarding learning and growth. Here is a small sample:

➢ We feel to express ourselves and tap into our deepest creative potential. We believe in what we are doing and integrate our sense of purpose into who we are.

➢ We must be profitable in order to survive but our primary purpose is to contribute to a better life for everyone we touch. We do this by providing meaningful work, dignified employment, beneficial goods and services, and relationships of trust and caring that are at the foundations of a healthy community.

➢ Everyone who comes in contact with our organization— employees, customers, and suppliers, people asking for donations, journalists and reporters, public officials—leaves with the perception that we exist in order to be of service.

➢ People come from all over the world to learn about almost everything we do.

➢ We are inventing and rediscovering ways to work, constantly teaching them within and outside Zingerman's. We teach people to learn so they learn to teach. Many employees have come to work here especially to further their education, be it about food, people, or organizational development.

➢ When employees move on it is with a sense of self-confidence and with experiences they can use to better the next organization they are a part of.

➢ Education is one of our passions. The more we teach, the

more we learn. The more we teach, the more customers and staff are drawn to visit and shop with us. The more we teach and learn together, the more effectively we connect with each other, strengthen our culture, and improve the lives of everyone we interact with. We thrive on sharing information lavishly.[58]

As observers of the company, we can attest that the vision for 2020 has been mostly accomplished as we write in 2019.

At the end of our interview, Ari invited us to order dinner and to feel free to speak to any of the employees, which we did. Each employee radiated with positive energy. One young lady said that working at Zingerman's had changed her life. It had helped her create a much more positive relationship with her daughter and her mother. A young man, a student at the University of Michigan, was working at Zingerman's during the summer. He hoped to someday start his own business and expressed gratitude for the company. Both raved about their experience. Their work was meaningful, they were learning and growing, they were part of a collaborative whole, and the company was flourishing.

Summary

We learn from previous experience to make the standard principal–agent assumption that employees are people who work for monetary incentives and promotions. We do not see much of a role for learning and growth as things that agents want in this incentive system. But stimulation, learning, and growth are one basic need, which purpose-driven leaders understand and focus on. The learning has value in itself, but it also produces benefits. In purpose-driven organizations like Zingerman's, unusual practices that revolve around growth and learning end up producing trust, collaboration, and higher performance, which reduce the contracting frictions in the principal–agent model. Thus, the fifth step in creating a purpose-driven organization is to create a purpose-driven culture that stimulates leaning.

Getting Started: Tools and Exercises

Hold a discussion and structure it as follows:

Phase 1. Have everyone read the chapter.

Phase 2. Give everyone a list of the seven points in the Zingerman's vision as listed on page 141.

Phase 3. Have each person take a personal perspective and rank the seven planks in terms of desirability. Combine everyone's scores.

Phase 4. Starting with the most highly ranked plank, discuss the extent to which it reflects the culture of your organization.

Phase 5. Add any new planks that emerge from your discussion.

Phase 6. Make a list of actions that your organization could take that would create a purpose-driven culture focused on learning and growth.

CHAPTER TWELVE

STEP 6 Turn Midlevel Managers into Purpose-Driven Leaders

We have a friend who strives to be a positive, purpose-driven leader. She was invited to join a new company that has a purpose-driven culture. She asked to meet with us and discuss her opportunity. As she described the culture of the new organization, she kept saying she felt attracted to the company.

We asked her what it meant to feel attracted. She described her interview with one of the senior executives. Within 15 minutes she was engaged in an intimate and candid exploration of who he really was and who she really was. She asked him, "What draws you here?"

Tears came to his eyes. He said, "When I leave home in the morning, I feel that I am driving to my second home and my second family. I feel that I am part of a community that is serving a community."

When later she met with the CEO, he spoke of the mission and purpose of the organization and the challenges of making a meaningful difference in the community. She said, "Everyone talked to me from both their hearts and their heads."

She contrasted these authentic conversations with a transactional conversation that had taken place in her own organization that morning, a discussion about an important promotion in which a man could enter a role of great influence and make an extraordinary difference. When asked about whether he would be interested in the position, instead of exploring the possibility of impact, he made financial demands. As he did, she felt energy draining from her. She was not attracted to the self-interested actor; she was repelled.

The contrast made her aware that she had never before visited a large organization that was purpose driven. She continued to speak of "attraction" and of the "drawing power" of the company. In relationships and in cultures where people are so engaged that they speak from both their heads and their hearts, others are drawn in and tend to engage.

Almost as an afterthought, she said, "In my life I have been blessed to have a network of extraordinary, purpose-focused people. It occurred to me that if I do take the job, the company will not only get me, they will also get a mini army of connections. They will get the positive energy and the positive thoughts that flow from my network into me. I bring those precious resources with me."

She was making an important point: Purpose-driven people often find themselves in networks of purpose-driven people who are engaged with both their heads and their hearts. They attract one another. Purpose-driven organizations are composed of many people who feel the organization is a community of service. It is their "second home" and their "second family." So they are willing to take initiatives they might not otherwise take. As a result, these midlevel people become leaders who embody the purpose and bring energy to the community.

Conventional Organizations

Once in a focus group interview at a Fortune 100 company, a woman described a phenomenon we have observed for decades but have never articulated. She said, "We have 1,600 executives. They fall into three groups. There is a very small group of people who know how to lead. When I meet one of them, I immediately know they are a leader because I want to be like them. We then have a large group of managers who intellectually understand leadership but do not practice it. Finally, we have another small group of technically oriented people who cannot even conceive of leading."

The woman was accurately describing a pattern that occurs in numerous organizations. We have since shared the story with scores of executives and asked them why the middle group is so large. Each time we do this, the room goes quiet. Slowly answers come: "It is too hard." "Leadership is risky." "The culture prevents it."

No one ever responds, "She is wrong. In our organization every executive and every manager is a leader." Rather, with some cha-grin, they recognize the fact, and painfully they explain it.

In organizations we often make conventional assumptions, and we expect and accept self-interested, political posturing in the vast majority of authority figures. We call them leaders because they hold positions of authority. But they actually fall in the large middle group.

Why is this the dominant paradigm of leadership? The entire lead-ership development industry is inculcated with the notions of knowl-edge and skill, and leadership is seen as a practice about knowing and doing. The assumption facilitates a fruitful exchange between universities and corporations. Universities produce knowledge and skills, and corporations buy those things. Yet little changes. The vast middle group in every organization continues to manage.

Why? "It is too hard." "Leadership is risky." "The culture prevents it." But there are exceptions—organizations and leaders who do not fit this mold.

Conventional Culture and Purpose Work

As mentioned in chapter 5, we interviewed Jim Weddle, then CEO of Edward Jones, the financial services company. He told us that the company's purpose is not to make a profit, not to help clients decrease taxes or increase income. The purpose is to help individuals meet their most important financial goals like educating their children, preparing for retirement, or leaving a legacy. Company profit is simply a metric that indicates how well the purpose is being served.

This orientation has guided the company for decades. When it was first introduced, some partners left. They could not accept the unconventional notion that profit was not the organization's purpose. We have noticed this same pattern in other organizations. Today, that purpose is a magnet that attracts many new associates and partners to the company. They naturally want to be paid for their work, but they also want to belong to an organization of higher purpose.

The notion of purpose is also a magnet that attracts clients. When clients get assistance in clarifying what they really want and in aligning with their desired future, they feel well looked after. They become loyal, and this positive reaction feeds back to employees and sparks their growth.

Jim told us that associates and partners do not feel like manipulative salespeople but like servants to the best interests of clients. With this positive orientation, associates and partners begin to feel good about themselves and what they do. Success creates faith and hope. They begin to believe the company can reach millions of future clients. The associates and partners become deeply committed, and they act like owners. They transcend the assumptions of the traditional principal–agent perspective. They invest more in their work and in their organization. Each one of them is a purpose-driven leader, self-motivated by the higher purpose rather than getting their direction from above.

The higher purpose has resulted in the emergence of a strong culture. The culture helps people feel like owners and makes it possible for people to lead without getting orders from above because the purpose is the arbiter of all decisions. This empowering culture is seen as so valuable that the company works to preserve it. Recruitment is focused on finding people who fit the culture. In one case, there was a wait of two years in finding the right chief marketing officer.

Systems and processes also reflect the culture. The company provides bonus pools and profit sharing plans. It sees that associates are treated like partners. It treats ownership as an opportunity. Competitors are stunned to learn how much it spends on small-group employee appreciation trips. The company also makes an extraordinary investment to ensure that new people are successful.

The company also places a great emphasis on integrity. Jim told us that when a company really has purpose and values and crisis comes, the leaders act in unconventional ways. During the financial crisis of 2008, its volume and profits were shrinking. Instead of the conventional response of cutting salaries and people, the leaders at Edward Jones cut 15 percent out of other areas. They told people that the company was responsible to its clients and employees. Expenses would be cut, but no person would be financially penalized or let go. They preserved the covenant that was described earlier by Ricardo Levy and Rabbi Sacks.

What happened? After the cost cuts, the company did not have another unprofitable month. Furthermore, although years have passed since that time, the people still speak of how they were treated in the time of crisis. There is a level of trust that money cannot buy. It is attractive and permeates the culture.

An Opportunity

As great as the Edward Jones story is, we have to note where the sense of higher purpose emerged. In chapter 5 we mentioned the role of Peter Drucker. Drucker forced the CEO and others to stay on a topic they did not wish to engage with: organizational purpose.

This reluctance suggests a golden opportunity for you. If so many people in positions of authority do not understand the power of purpose and resist doing purpose work, you potentially have a great advantage. If you are willing to contemplate and experiment and learn to do purpose work at whatever level you occupy, you can become a rare and desired asset, a positive leader who can create a purpose-driven culture.

While the opportunity to do purpose work is available to every midlevel person, few will embrace it. A challenge for senior leaders who seek to create a purpose-driven organization is to turn midlevel professionals into leaders. In fact, until this happens, an organization will not be a purpose-driven community. Senior people tend to understand this as a concept, but they do not tend to embrace it. They are sometimes hindered by not knowing what to do or by an unwillingness to invest the necessary resources. Yet as they themselves become purpose driven, a new vision unfolds.

We turn now to a company where such a vision emerged and midlevel managers became purpose-driven leaders.

The Evolution of Leadership in an Unlikely Place

A Big Four accounting firm is a cooperative made up of thousands of partners.[59] The partners think like accountants: They tend to be careful in their observations, exact in their assessments, and cautious about their decisions. They tend to have a conservative culture, and they are not inclined to get emotional about abstractions. Changing the culture of any company is difficult; changing the culture of an accounting firm is a true challenge.

In 2004 the culture at KPMG was becoming an issue of concern. Surveys showed that only 50 percent of the employees thought the culture was favorable. Turnover was in the high 20 percent range. A variety of typical HR programs were used to raise favorability scores, which climbed into the 80 percent range. Bruce Pfau, vice chair of HR at KPMG, said, "It was an accomplishment, but we had a problem: we desired higher scores and we were out of programs and out of ideas." Bruce needed to think in a new way. He soon had some random experiences that provided new perspectives and led to two actions right away.

First, Bruce got exposed to the data. There was an item on the satisfaction survey that continually showed up with low scores: "My job has special meaning." Bruce believed that nothing could be done about meaning, yet the challenge stayed with him. He then had a conversation with a management professor who told him a story about the CEO of Men's Wearhouse. The CEO sincerely believed that the mission of the company was not to sell suits but to help people genuinely feel better. This higher purpose seemed to permeate the organization. The idea of higher purpose also stayed with Bruce.

Second, Bruce visited an actuarial firm. In the foyer of the office was an exhibit of memorabilia from the firm's history. As he talked with people, he heard them express pride in their organization's past. At KPMG history was seldom discussed, and culture was not seen as a lever of performance. Bruce began to ask, "At KPMG, what is our highest purpose?"

In the meantime, John Veihmeyer, the former chair of the US division, was coming to a similar viewpoint. He told us that, as chair of the US division, he knew he was not doing "the one thing that had the most potential to change the organization: increase employee engagement."

John recognized that the leadership of the firm was not deeply connected with the people. They were not tapping the potential of the organization, and employees tended to make only incremental improvements.

Soon KPMG launched an effort to find the company's higher purpose. As we have said, an organization does not invent a higher purpose—it discovers it. In this case, the whole organization got involved in the discovery, which made it easier to connect the people to the discovered purpose. They conducted hundreds of interviews and analyzed the responses. Eventually, they distilled the information into a few words. They found the purpose of KPMG: to "Inspire Confidence and Empower Change."

The senior people were excited. At this point, many companies would have given in to the next, natural temptation. They would have announced the higher purpose and marketed it inside and outside the firm. Both John and Bruce knew this would be a grand mistake.

An organization finds its higher purpose with a goal to inspire and unify, to connect people to the whole. They do not accomplish this through typical administrative techniques. They must follow the principles of authenticity and constancy. People need to believe that the collective purpose is real. They need to see a link between the collective purpose and what they personally do.

So KPMG asked a new question and launched a new initiative. The new question was "What do you do at KPMG?" and the answer was captured in a video, "We shape history." It turned out that KPMG had a rich past that was largely forgotten. Among other things, the company had assisted in managing the Lend-Lease Act that help defeat Nazi Germany. It was instrumental in bringing about the release of US hostages in Iran. It certified the election of Nelson Mandela. The company could look back on many great accomplishments, and it began to recognize and celebrate them.

Evolving

John and Bruce came to believe that their midlevel managers, trained in accounting, must become purpose-driven leaders. This, however, was a big ask, and resistance was natural. In the meantime, John and Bruce also continued to evolve.

John identified a key learning experience. In their early efforts to find purpose and connect people to it, he did what Nick Craig warned us about. He brought in a consulting firm to help with the purpose work. Following conventional assumptions, the firm directed them to do work that was analytical and intellectual. The firm spent months doing what their KPMG client expected, clarifying definitions of words like *purpose, vision, mission, ethos,* and *culture.* They did not get understanding and engagement, only confusion and boredom.

Frustrated, Bruce told John that he was not interested in having people do a structural analysis of "The Star-Spangled Banner." He was interested in having people *sing* "The Star-Spangled Banner." He saw all the analytical work as a distraction, a form of work avoidance. Just as Bruce's mind was opened to a new perspective by his random experiences, John's mind was opened by this unexpected statement. He said, "Bruce's words unlocked me!"

John could see how the conventional perspective usually leads to a lack of engagement. He also knew that leadership is about trust. A leader cannot move an organization if the people do not trust the leader.

When John was leading the relatively small Washington, DC, unit, he made a point of constantly being with his people. They knew him, and they trusted him. When John became chair of the entire US operation, suddenly he was leading 2,000 partners who did not know him or trust him.

Intuitively, John knew he had to establish trust, but he had no idea how to solve the problems of distance and time. Shortly after Bruce made the comment about singing instead of analyzing, John began to experiment with risk taking of another form: establishing intimacy by his own storytelling and authentic expression. Like Gerry Anderson, like Jimmy Dunne, and like so many others we have featured in this book, John saw the need to increase his own authenticity and vulnerability.

John was about to deliver a major address to the 2,000 partners. He was determined to give a unique talk: He would reveal himself. He would tell the partners why he loved the firm and what he believed about the purpose of his life and the purpose of the firm. Then the conventional culture stepped in. Some of the people around him were appalled by the idea and tried to dissuade John.

John mustered his courage, and he gave the talk. He told stories of seeing people in the firm do remarkable things. He told them why he was at the firm, what the purpose of the firm meant to him. He said that there was a need for "a different kind of conversation." People needed emotional connections with the partners and the partners needed to share their authentic selves. They needed to tell their people why they loved the firm. Accounting is hard work. There are some bad days, and on those days, people need to know why they are getting out of bed in the morning.

Creating Purpose-Driven Leaders

John got feedback that was wildly positive, and the talk became a landmark moment. He said it was "cathartic" for everyone present. "What I was really doing was beginning to create a culture that gave them permission to fully engage as whole human beings. I was giving the partners permission to be who they really are. I was inviting them to create a new kind of conversation. I was asking them to do to their people what I had just done to them."

The partners were impressed by the message, but they were still accountants who were coming from the conventional mind-set. We can think about what John invited them to do: create a different kind of conversation, make emotional connections, share their authentic selves, tell why they loved the firm, and give people a reason to get out of bed in the morning. This is not the usual work of managers. It is the work of purpose-driven leaders. John and Bruce knew they had to turn managers into what they were not, and it was not enough to simply ask them to take that on. They knew the partners would need help.

The company hired an outside firm to train the partners in how to tell their intimate stories and share their purpose. It was difficult work, but success stories began to emerge. Today, partners communicate their personal purpose and discuss how it links to their professional lives. In doing so, they are speaking from a courageous place and modeling authenticity and vulnerability. They are giving their people permission to be whole. They are cascading a purpose-driven, positive culture throughout the firm.

Summary

In the principal–agent model, the CEO is the leader who plays the role of the principal, and midlevel managers are agents. The organization presumes that purpose leadership is the CEO's task. Thus, it does not see the task of purpose leadership shared by midlevel managers. However, when the organization embraces an authentic higher purpose, it sees a surprising pattern emerge. Midlevel employees take on the role of the principal and become leaders who turn the culture into a system that attracts people to it.

But this role for midlevel managers is not common. We find it counterintuitive to think that midlevel managers, who typically do not have stock options and large chunks of stock ownership in the firm, would behave as if they were ownership-motivated leaders. The sixth counterintuitive step in creating a purpose-driven organization is to turn middle managers into authentic, purpose-driven leaders who act like owners.

Getting Started: Tools and Exercises

Hold a discussion and structure it as follows:

Phase 1. Have everyone read the chapter and write answers to the following questions:

➢ How many of our people drive to work feeling they are headed to their second home and second family?

➢ How many of the people in our executive and management workforce are purpose-driven leaders?

> ➤ Identify an outstanding example of a purpose-driven leader and describe what they do differently in relating to others.

> ➤ Why do many people avoid purpose work?

> ➤ In terms of developing midlevel managers, what principles are to be found in the KPMG case?

Phase 2. As a group discuss the answers to the above questions and develop a set of guidelines for turning midlevel managers into purpose-driven leaders.

CHAPTER THIRTEEN

STEP 7 Connect the People to the Purpose

We flew to Atlanta to work with six people from a company that is trying to execute change and move into the future. When we work with companies, we try to introduce the basic concepts and tools from our work in positive organizational scholarship and the economics of higher purpose.

Often, we find the going tough because executives are suspicious of ideas that violate their conventional expectations. In Atlanta we had the opposite experience. The people immediately took in the ideas and extended them in creative ways. It was a joyful experience.

This willing reception came about because the people had previously lived through and benefited from a positive transformation. Their unconventional experience had already predisposed them to the positive and inclusive mind-set.

The company, Interface, makes flexible floor coverings including carpet tiles. In 1994 the CEO, Ray Anderson, had an unusual experience. Here is his account of what happened as he prepared to speak to a group of professionals:

> Frankly, I didn't have a vision, except "comply, comply, comply."
> I sweated for three weeks over what to say to that group. Then,

through what seemed like pure serendipity, somebody sent me a book, Paul Hawken's *The Ecology of Commerce.* I read it, and it changed my life. It was an epiphany. I wasn't halfway through it before the vision I sought became clear, along with a powerful sense of urgency to do something. . . . I agreed with his central thesis. . . . Business is the largest, wealthiest, most pervasive institution on Earth, and responsible for most of the damage. It must take the lead in directing the Earth away from collapse, and toward sustainability.[60]

As result of this experience, Anderson determined to maintain his business goals while also leading the world in industrial ecology (being friendly to the planet). He had gone through a paradigm shift. Acting on it required courageous leadership.

Everyone in the company believed that Anderson had lost his mind. When he gave his first public speech about his intention, the people outside the company agreed. Investors also seemed to agree: the stock price fell 40 percent in one day. The company entered a dark valley. But it nonetheless began to move forward, building the bridge as it walked on it.

Since that time, the company has grown into a billion-dollar operation that does business in 110 countries. It became one of the Forbes Most Admired Companies in America and one of the Forbes 100 Best Companies to Work For. One executive told us the Interface story in detail. He kept saying, with emphasis, "It was a miracle. I lived through it, and it was a miracle."

One of the women present understood the concepts of emergence and self-organization and she responded: "I am not sure it was a miracle. We had a purpose, and we made connections. When you make connections, new things grow. You flourish."

In her short statement, she captured the essence of why it is important to connect employees to the higher purpose of the organization. When the organization is connected to an authentic higher purpose, culture changes, and people empower themselves to do the right thing. As they move forward, they collectively learn to do what was not previously possible. The organization flourishes because the people go into accelerated collective and individual learning. Afterward, they sometimes lack the language to conceptualize what took place.

While they may lack the language, they do have the memory. When they hear the concepts related to organizational higher purpose and positive organizing, they are able to extend and apply the concepts. This is why the Interface session was so generative. People who have experienced higher purpose and positive organizing are more prepared to accept the concepts associated with creating positive organizations. They are anxious to increase collaboration.

As the Interface example suggests, a major challenge is getting the people at the lower levels to envision and understand the highest purpose, getting them, the agents, to act like Ray Anderson, the principal. In the last chapter, we examined the process of enrolling midlevel managers into higher purpose. Few companies do this. In this chapter, we examine the process of bringing the entire workforce, particularly first-line people, to higher purpose. Fewer companies do this. We begin with the insights of a man who has spent his life shrink-wrapping corporate speak.

Shrink-Wrapping Corporate Speak

Jim Haudan is the chairman of Root Inc., a consulting firm that focuses on purpose and engagement. Root has gifted artists who take 300-page strategic plans and turn them into a few pictures. This is a process of massive simplification. The people at Root use the pictures to engage people in authentic discussions that become both interesting and generative.

Jim says that many executives think they are imbuing the organization with purpose when they formulate and communicate a corporate strategy. Typically, brilliant people at the top spend months analyzing and reducing complexity. Then they formulate a plan.

Members of the senior team, with help from corporate communications, make presentations of the strategy to people at lower levels. But not much happens; the emphasis is on presentation.

The frustrated executives think, "If the people could see what we see, they would behave differently." This is actually a sound assumption—they *would* behave differently. The unfortunate truth is that the people do not see what the executives see because executives cannot communicate what they see. What they see is a right-brained vision. What they communicate, however, is a left-brained set of words. The words lack authentic passion and the clinical communication of strategy leaves people cold.

Jim says that moving communication from the linear left brain to the visual right brain reduces vast amounts of complexity. The process of visualization helps people discover, simplify, and communicate the purpose. "When they have a simple visual they begin to see the purpose, they show childlike zeal, they open up and they are willing to learn."

Jim tells the story of a major company that had not met its financial plan for several years. It was in the process of transforming from a carbonated soft drink company to a total beverage company. Everything at every level was going to have to change. For example, the unionized truck drivers would have to become salespeople. It was a huge shift in expectations.

Jim ran a meeting that included a truck driver named Bob. Bob's every other word seemed to begin with *F.* From the first moment, Bob made it clear that he was not going to cooperate. Jim put up a simple visual that reduced pages of strategy and showed how the business was going to work. As people examined it, Bob walked over. He suddenly volunteered the information that 55 percent of what was on the truck each day came back. He pointed out that 40 percent of the invoices were wrong. He began to scream about the incompetence of management and how it was going to cost everyone their jobs.

Then one of Bob's peers interrupted him and explained that the entire process was undermined by the fact that every day there was a stack of information sheets that Bob threw in the garbage. In fact, he had just done that very thing. Bob stood in stunned silence. Then he said, "Give me back those sheets."

In a matter of minutes, Bob, the unreachable resister, discovered how what he was doing was affecting the business, and that discovery changed his attitude. Bob was transformed and became an engaged employee. The process was extended to 32,000 people, and the entire company transformed.

Jim told us that when transformative learning takes place at the bottom of an organization, it loops back to the top of the organization. When executives see radical change at the bottom, it challenges their existing assumptions. Often the conventional mind-set crumbles, and the positive mind-set emerges. Executives suddenly see resources they never knew existed.

In this case, the CEO and his team were "dumbfounded" when they discovered the untapped potential in their people. The CEO said, "You know, we've spent the last 10 years trying to teach them how to do a better job, assuming they would improve the business. But we never thought to share the business with them and let them take control of improving it."

They had never thought to do that because the idea is counterintuitive. A woman from HR, who was in charge of the process and witnessed the meetings, also explained the executive transformation. She said, "It was welcome to the church." By this she meant that the senior executives experienced a conversion, a shift from the conventional mind-set to the positive, inclusive mind-set. It was the same transformation we have seen throughout this book.

Sounding like the above woman from Interface, who understands the power of connections in the emergent process, she went on to say, "We pigeonholed folks according to our perception of their limitations. *They had no way to be engaged because we were preventing it.* Then, after years, we clarified the purpose, and we watched them connect and come alive. They were full of potential. We had resources in the organization that we could not see and that we had never before tapped."

We could extend the woman's assertion to almost all large organizations. Executives look down at the hierarchy and see many people who bring only their bodies to work. Given what they see, these executives make an assumption that only partially reflects reality. They come to believe that the people in the organization are agents who seek to minimize their personal costs, people who will not engage and bring their discretionary energy to work.

When executives act on their assumptions, they create organizations that are based on the notion of transactional exchange. They seek to control people by designing systems of external rewards and punishments. "We will give you money and other rewards, and you will do what is in your job description."

This basic assumption turns people into robots, yet people do not want to be robots. Seeing no other alternative, they disengage, and a few put their creative energy into disrupting the organization. They become like Bob the truck driver, who threw away his forms. When executives witness this kind of disruption, they make another flawed but comfortable assumption: "The fault is in the people."

The inclusive, or positive, mental model is more complex than the conventional mental model. It recognizes that the dynamics we've described exist, but it does not put the fault in the people. It does not put the fault anywhere. Instead, it focuses on the purpose and on the strengths of the people and on the fact that, under the right circumstances, they can become genuinely committed and connected and willing to go the extra mile.

Jim told us that organizations need leaders who can "shrink-wrap" the complexity of "corporate speak" and give the people a picture or a metaphor that allows them to see and understand the whole system in a simple way. When people at any level come to understand the whole system, they become whole people who begin to connect to other whole people. The social network becomes a system of positive energy, learning, and adaptation. When this happens, reality challenges conventional theory. Executives begin to see that their organizations are filled with resources they could not previously see. Jim's approach of simplifying and visualizing is a practical way to connect people to the higher purpose as well as to the strategy of the organization.

Reaching Everyone

Creating a purpose-driven organization is a great challenge. It requires understanding and implementing many principles that are counterintuitive. It means seeing the principal–agent problem as the principal–agent *opportunity*. It means believing that people want to contribute. It means taking the responsibility to extend this transformation all the way to the bottom of the organization.

In chapter 12 we examined the evolution of KPMG and how the firm turned its midlevel managers into purpose-driven leaders.[61] The story continues as KPMG did something that few organizations ever do. It reached everyone.

Bruce and John saw the need for a bottom-up effort. People needed to see their own purpose and how that purpose can get realized at work. They encouraged people to share their own accounts of how they were currently making a difference. This effort evolved into a remarkable program called the 10,000 Stories Challenge.

The program gave the 27,000 employees access to a digital program and invited them to create posters. In the process, it asked them to answer the question "What do you do at KPMG?" It then asked them to write a headline such as "I Combat Terrorism."

For example, under the headline "I Combat Terrorism" are statements such as "KPMG helps scores of financial institutions prevent money laundering, keeping financial resources out of the hands of terrorists and criminals." Under the statement is a picture of the author. Finally, the poster reads; "Inspire Confidence. Empower Change."

In June the company announced that if 10,000 posters were submitted by Thanksgiving, it would add two extra days to the Christmas break. For the leadership of an accounting firm, this was a risky undertaking. As is almost always the case in initiating a positive culture, many people believed the entire process would be seen as "corny," no one would respond, and the leaders would be left embarrassed. The leaders spent considerable time debating about moving forward.

Nearly all leaders who desire to create a positive culture experience genuine fear. They need courage to overcome that fear, as we have seen in earlier chapters. When they succeed in such an effort, they are often euphoric.

The program at KPMG produced a shocking outcome: The 10,000 stories were produced in a month, and the people earned their two days off. Not only that, but the process went viral. Although the reward was already earned, the posters continued to appear: 27,000 people submitted 42,000 posters (some people submitted multiple times, and teams submitted as well as individuals). It turned out that the people of KPMG had a pent up appetite for purpose and meaning. The company had found a brilliant way to help the people connect the collective purpose and their individual purpose.

Did all the work on purpose matter, and did it affect performance? The company's surveys showed that pride increased, engagement scores went to record levels, good-place-to-work scores jumped from 82 percent to 89 percent. KPMG climbed 17 places in Fortune's Best Companies to Work For list, making KPMG the highest-ranked firm of the Big Four. It saw its turnover go down dramatically, generating advantages in terms of continuity, recruiting, training, and comprehensive savings. While we cannot show a causal link, we can note that the firm had an outstanding financial year and also achieved the highest growth rate of the Big Four accounting firms.

A Warning

We've seen the work by Jim Haudan in the beverage company and by executives at KPMG that provide brilliant examples of approaches for taking purpose to the bottom of the organization. You might yearn for tools that you could implement with minimal reflection and minimal risk.

We wish to warn you that in nearly every case in this book we have learned of leaders having to enter uncertainty and learn how to create a purpose-driven organization. Human systems are not technical systems; they are complex, living systems, as are all individual human beings and collections of human beings.

When the connections between the parts of a system elevate in quality, new collective properties emerge. When an individual like Shauri finds her personal higher purpose, she integrates her heart and mind, and a new, more integrated and authentic self-emerges. Sharui then becomes a leader. When a leader invites people to a higher purpose and they accept, the quality of connections in the network changes and new properties emerge.

The process is not linear. The process is not controllable. Initiating the process requires both the inviter and the invited to engage in a journey of learning from experience. The journey seems to contradict many assumptions that hold in the conventional mindset. To create a purpose-driven organization, you need the courage to learn while stimulating learning as it is happening in real time.

Learning While Stimulating Learning

The field of positive organizational scholarship was born at the University of Michigan's Ross School of Business.[62] Ross has spawned much research on how to create organizations of higher purpose, organizations where people flourish in positive cultures and exceed expectations.

Amy Byron-Oilar, who was hired as chief people officer (head of HR) at Ross, was exposed to such ideas and determined to apply some of the research by building a positive work community. Amy and the dean of the school agreed that the principles of positive organizing should be applied inside the school.

Years later, we talked with Amy about the initiatives that were launched. The process started with two efforts in 2011, and the number increased every year. Yet Amy pointed out that the process was not so linear or systematic. What emerged was not the result of a conventional master plan. She said that what was done in subsequent years "could not be imagined in the previous years." The process was an emergent one that required purpose, courage, and learning.

Consider this unusual statement: "I wanted a plan. I tried to write a plan . . . over and over. That's what we're taught. Figure out where you are. Determine where you need to be. Chart your path. Execute, and, voilà, success! It was part of my personal journey to let that thinking go."

In Amy's first year, she encountered high levels of staff dissatisfaction. So in 2011, at the suggestion of the dean, she established a staff involvement group with representatives from all areas of the school. This effort eventually gave rise in 2012 to a community learning group inspired by faculty research on the importance of learning in creating positive cultures. That group spawned mini-conferences that explored best practices and resulted in lists of "tips, tricks and new great stuff." That in turn spawned better staff meetings, a staff lounge, and the return of a popular past practice called Green Clean, in which all members of the workforce were invited to participate in a day for deep cleaning the buildings.

In 2013 faculty and staff members worked with a Zingerman's training group (see chapter 11) to create a future vision. This seemingly small act clarified purpose and legitimized creating a positive future, and it empowered people. Suddenly people felt that they could create new initiatives.

One initiative began when a few people were trained and certified in teaching a program on crucial conversations. Then 150 members of the staff were trained. The staff had long complained of a lack of respect from faculty, and in one discussion, someone proposed that the solution might be for staff to increase their own respect for faculty. This led to a classroom observation program where staff could sit in on classes and see both faculty and students at their best. And it led to a comprehensive onboarding process to expose new employees to every aspect of life in the school.

In 2014 a campus-wide effort toward "shared services" affected the staff of the business school. Many staff members were interviewed, and it became clear that they did not feel connected to one another or to the school. This led to a networking effort including bimonthly community-building exercises.

Another initiative launched a selection boot camp that was run by staff to help other staff hire people more likely to contribute to the positive vision. An initiative put in place an annual health rally, and another one redesigned the performance appraisal tool to foster positive knowledge, skills, and abilities.

In 2015 HR developed specific new modules for the onboarding process. Every other month the department selected a staff member and profiled the person to the entire school. With the new shared services program in place, many people were suddenly sharing workspaces, and this turned out to be as likely to generate conflict as it did cooperation. HR put in place a program to help people cooperate. It created a video that captured what it means to create and live in a positive community.

HR also developed a related program on knowledge and practice sharing. Faculty members published a new edited book on developing positive leadership, and the department invited individual faculty authors to teach various chapters to the staff.

HR recruited staff members to help share the positive vision with new staff by speaking about their own positive stories and experiences. Finally, it created a vision statement that contained many aspirations such as "Operate with the positive end in mind" and "See the good in others." It turned these aspirations into an assessment tool so people could analyze themselves individually or collectively and explore avenues for their improvement. With all these efforts, the department intended to convert everybody in the organization into purpose-driven leaders in a way that had not been experienced before.

In 2016 we met with Amy again. She shared with us the results of a recent employee engagement survey. The gains were large, and changes on 17 indicators were statistically significant. The producers of the report said they had never before seen a shift of such magnitude.

As Amy reflected on this achievement, she returned to the notion of emergence. She said, "Someone recently suggested that we create a video about the faculty like the one we did about the staff. Two years ago it would have been impossible to have that idea. Every time we do something, it creates new possibilities. The process keeps expanding; we are learning our way forward."

We asked Amy about the impact of the achievement on her. She said, "Early on, I attended an executive education course on positive leadership given by our faculty. One of them taught me to ask, 'What would you do if you had 2 percent more courage?' Over and over, I have asked that question because building a positive work community requires courage. The impact on me has been very real. I am amazed, and my thinking has expanded immeasurably. I can do things now that would have been impossible at the start."

Amy has learned how to create a purpose-driven, positive organization inside a business school by creating a culture that invites everyone to commit to a higher purpose. Creating a purpose-driven organization required leadership, the courage to embrace a purpose, and the ability to involve the top, the middle, and the bottom levels of the organization.

Summary

It is not enough for an organization to simply discover an authentic higher purpose. The organization has to connect the purpose to the people and their emotions. Both middle managers (chapter 12) and first-line employees have to take ownership of the purpose and be energized by it. Connecting the purpose to the people requires leaders to act in ways that contradict their basic assumptions about how they should behave in organizations.

Some leaders learn to do this. They transcend convention and provide leadership we do not expect to see. They communicate an inspiring and authentic vision in ways that help people find their purpose and the organization's purpose. Purpose-driven leaders understand the importance of doing this, for everyone including those at the bottom of the organization. Thus, the seventh counterintuitive step in creating a purpose-driven organization is to discover the possibility of connecting first-line people to the higher purpose of the organization. In other words, the seventh step is to connect the people to the purpose.

Getting Started: Tools and Exercises

Hold a discussion and structure it as follows:

Phase 1. Have everyone read the chapter.

Phase 2. Have everyone write answers to these questions:

➢ What do you understand about purpose, connections, and emergence?

➢ What key principles can we derive from Jim Haudan's work at the beverage company?

➢ What key principles can we derive from the implementation of higher purpose at KPMG?

➢ What key principles can we derive from Amy's journey at the business school?

Phase 3. Discuss the answers and review the list of guidelines for engaging middle managers that you created in chapter 12. Now jointly create a list of guidelines for engaging all the people.

CHAPTER FOURTEEN

STEP 8 Unleash the Positive Energizers

One day we ran into an old friend who directs human resources in a large organization. We inquired as to how she was doing, and she told us that things were not going very well at work. The people at the top faced difficult challenges and were responding in conventional ways. They were becoming increasingly negative, and the negativity was flowing through the organization.

We asked her to consider a counterintuitive question: What would happen if she went back to her organization and selected people whom she knew were inherently positive, committed to the collective good, and competent? What if she invited them to become a network of positive change agents? What if she assembled them and asked them what they wanted the organization to look like in the future? What if she asked them what they could do to bring that vision into reality?

We asked these questions based on our experience. Every organization has a pool of purpose-driven people. The pool often goes unrecognized. We refer to this pool as "the invisible network of positive energizers." Spread randomly throughout the organization, positive energizers are mature, purpose-driven people with an optimistic orientation, people like Corey Mundle, whom we described in chapter 7. They are open and willing to take initiative, and they naturally energize others. Once invited, they can assist with culture change. These people are easy to identify, they radiate positive energy, and they are trusted.

Our proposal was not a conventional one. For our friend, it raised many immediate concerns, but it did intrigue her. It gave her a small ray of hope at a dark time. We told her to go home and sleep on the idea, then give us a call so we could discuss it.

She did call. She said that, on the one hand, something about our proposal seemed radical and uncomfortable. It did not conform to the conventional assumption that all change efforts should be directed from the top and flow down the hierarchy. On the other hand, she suggested that it was her responsibility to lead the way in creating a better culture. She concluded that taking care of the people in the company was not only her job; it was at the heart of her personal purpose. She concluded that she was going to move ahead because it was the right thing to do.

She had already held two meetings. She reported that she was overwhelmed by the interest and commitment of the people who had assembled. They were "fellow travelers" who felt as strongly as she did, and they were willing to go the extra mile to accomplish something. They were an amazing resource that until now had gone unrecognized. Moreover, she no longer felt alone.

The group analyzed the current state of the organization and then the desired state of the organization. On the one hand, the company was full of inherently good people who were loyal, ethical, dedicated, proud, and hungry to collaborate and win. The people knew they were surrounded by external opportunities, they recognized that the company was at a crossroads, and they were anxious to see the company succeed.

On the other hand, the people were full of anxiety. They saw that the competitiveness of the company was in question, that the focus was only on metrics, that there was no unifying vision, that confusion and conflict were increasing, that people were becoming increasingly territorial and fragmented, that fear permeated the organization, that people tended to be trapped in their old ways, that blame and finger pointing were increasing. They felt that there was a growing sense of exhaustion, and people were not anxious to get out of bed in the morning.

The group wanted to have a successful, competitive, growing company, with a clear mission and purpose. The company would be customer focused and always changing. It would have a learning culture. It would emphasize clarity, trust, candor, and collaboration. It would have people who were confident, innovative, energized, and empowered high performers making speedy decisions. It would be profitable because the people were committed to growing the profit margin.

This vision exhilarated the group of positive energizers. They were anxious to take the next step, but they were not sure what that was. Our friend invited us to meet with the group. We asked the group to teach us who they were and what they really valued. For an hour they talked with enthusiasm. We then asked them to make a list of the most important questions they wanted us to answer. They asked very thoughtful questions that fell into two categories: how should they personally and collectively operate so as to make a difference?

Personal Versus Collective Purpose

We engaged the group in an exploration of both themes. We suggested that they each needed a statement of personal purpose. They needed to align everything they did with their personal purpose. This notion was well received.

We then spoke of how they could, at their level, help their people to find their personal purpose, and their collective purpose, and connect the two. We discussed the positively deviant patterns that might arise and become contagious across the organization. They liked this notion but expressed considerable fear about the reaction from above.

At this point, our friend said she would like to share her personal journey. For 10 minutes she told an intimate story about her fears, her desires, and her decisions. The story was moving, and the people in the room were genuinely inspired.

We asked them, "What were the most important points in the story?" They came up with many answers but missed what we thought was the most important. At one moment in her account, our friend told of an incident with one of the senior people. She gave him a general description of what she was doing with the positive energizers. He responded, "Oh, I like that. I think it is good that there is an organic effort to improve things and that we do not have to try to generate it from the top."

We asked the group to focus on those words and share their insights. When they were done sharing, we summarized: "So what you are saying is that you already have a license from the top. By meeting in this group, you are simply doing your jobs as leaders in this company. You are not here leading a rebellion against authority. You are here leading a rebellion against the failure of this organization. You are helping the people above you do what they desire. You are positive deviants, not negative deviants. If you frame what you are doing incorrectly, you may offend the people above, but if you frame what you are doing carefully, they will likely welcome your effort. So how do you move forward effectively?"

They seemed inspired, and they shared ideas. One woman then raised her hand and said that she wanted to share something she might not normally share. She said that recently there was a challenge in the company. Ninety percent of the units in the field met the difficult challenge successfully. The immediate reaction of her boss was to ignore the efforts of the 90 percent and figure out ways to push the 10 percent to do better. She was incensed and took a stand. She described how she then effectively worked to turn the attention of her boss from the failing 10 percent to the celebration of what the 90 percent had accomplished.

At the perfect moment, this soft-spoken woman gave us a model at the personal level that this group of positive energizers could pursue at the collective level. It was a profound moment. A group of change agents was engaged in a learning relationship in which they were discovering how to empower themselves to act and carry purpose and positive culture into and up the organization.

Her example illustrated that transformative change begins on the inside. If you want to positively influence your leaders or peers, you need to do what they and others are afraid to do. You need to have the courage to put the collective good ahead of your ego needs. Doing so is the essence of leadership. When you are purpose-driven, you find the ability to envision and do what is normally impossible to envision and do.

We had created a space where the positive energizers could meet and learn and empower themselves. Every positive energizer in the room would have to do the same. Leadership is not about directing other people. It is about providing a relationship that allows others to learn and grow and do what they could not previously do. It is also about each person's own demonstration of courage and commitment. As people step out of the comfort zone and into the role of the positive deviant, they model what others can also do.

As people yearn to bring positive organizing to those above them or across from them, they are yearning for others to have the courage to be positive deviants, to do good things that are outside the conventional culture. Like them, they are filled with fear, which is justified. They know that deviance is risky. They know that they have legions of managers who hold hierarchical positions, but they have very few leaders who wield transformative influence.

The step of forming a group of positive energizers is useful because the energizers are individually and collectively predisposed to understand the positive lens. We almost always suggest to CEOs who want to create a purpose-driven organization that they should engage a network of positive energizers.

Positive Energizers at DTE Energy

We have helped launch networks of positive energizers in numerous organizations. Typically, in the first meeting, senior leaders invite network members to become involved in the design and the execution of the change process. Within minutes, they achieve buy in. The members of the network schedule regular meetings. They go out into the company, share ideas, and return with feedback and new ideas. One of the companies we have worked with is DTE Energy, which has created a network of positive energizers and turned the idea into a high art form.

We attended the first meeting of the positive energizer network. At the outset, the senior leader greeted the members of the network. He reviewed the history, explained that they were being asked to guide culture change, that there was no map, that they were in uncharted waters, that they were being asked to envision, dream, and create. He asked them to introduce themselves and gave them three tasks. They were to introduce themselves, explain how they access positive energy, and share their favorite vacation spot.

After the introductions, we asked the people to reflect on what people had said and identify the unusual commonalities. People said that the members were authentic and comfortably vulnerable. Individuals, for example, openly spoke of the challenges overcome by their parents or children or themselves. One man said his father grew up in a tent, came to the United States with nothing, and was now a professor. When he pondered this fact, he became confident that he could do what needed to be done in life. Another spoke of the commitment of having a handicapped child, and the blessings to the family. He inspired us all with his story.

These were optimistic people. Many shared personal life challenges but expressed genuine gratitude for the benefits that they associated with the challenges.

They also observed that the group found meaning in their work. A union member said, "I have been a lineman for over 20 years, but I have never worked a day in my life. I love what I do, and I love the people I work with."

They said the group was about relationships because the participants had much to say about helping others and learning from others. They said the group was curious because many spoke of vacations as learning experiences. Finally, they focused on the learning of others. One man, for example, joyfully described his daughter and her constant progress in soccer. Another spoke of seeing herself as a teacher at work and rejoiced in the development of her people.

Formulating a Vision

As the session closed, we realized that DTE had assembled a whole network of people like Corey Mundle. They were positive energizers who were ready to own their work. What they did over the next few months was impressive.

A Statement of Vision

First, they worked on their own purpose as a collective and created a grounded vision statement of what might occur in the next 18 months. Like at Zingerman's, they wrote their statement as if they were looking back in time. Here is their vision:

Wednesday, December 19, 2018

It's hard to believe it has been 18 months since the Positive Energizer Network [PEN] kickoff event at Copeley Hill. As a group, we've made so much progress, and we can see our work taking hold throughout DTE Energy. We have helped DTE evolve in its understanding of being a positive organization. It is now well understood that being a part of a purpose-driven, positive organization does not mean "being nice" but rather is defined by valuing both results and relationships, focusing on the "how" and "why" behind results, and not just the "what."

This afternoon, the network is getting together for one of our regular meetings, and I look forward to this meeting, as it energizes me and gives me a chance to connect with the colleagues I don't get to see that often.

I can remember our first meeting and how we all weren't sure what this network was all about and we were challenged to deal with this ambiguity. We still get a good laugh when we tell new members about our "blind tent-building" activity from the 2017 kickoff retreat. But over the last 18 months we've realized that "building the bridge as we walk on it" is energizing, especially when doing this within a close-knit community like the PEN network. We went from ambiguity to developing a clear purpose that guides us in positively impacting individuals, teams, and the enterprise.

In the last year and a half, we have taken trips to visit other organizations that practice positive leadership. We have visited Menlo Innovations in Ann Arbor, and Cascade Engineering in Grand Rapids, and we have more visits planned in the year ahead.

Last May, 80 percent of our network members attended the Positive Business Conference at the Ross School of Business. We identified three key learnings that we applied at DTE, and are showing positive results now that we are over six months out.

Not only have we been learning from others; we now have the chance to teach and share what we've accomplished. Because we did a great job of documenting the experiments and working together as a team, we are in talks with Ross to present our own session at the Positive Business Conference in 2019. We are also on the agenda for the 2019 meeting for all leaders in the company.

Accomplishments in the first 18 months: We've grown—we

started with a group of about 20 of us, and now we are nearing
40. This growth is the result of inviting other natural energizers
whom we've met and who expressed an interest in this work. We've
managed the growth so that we are able to maintain the cohesive-
ness of the group. The network meets every four to six weeks,
with 90 percent of members able to attend either in person or via
Skype. Network subgroups meet more frequently, using the time to
experiment in areas that they are passionate about.

We were also able to launch network nodes this past summer—
15 of the original PEN members took the initiative to build new
networks in their business units, ranging in size from 5 to 25, and
expand the impact of our work. During meetings, we share and
swap success stories related to what's been happening in our own
areas.

One of our biggest contributions to date has been teaching other
leaders and individual contributors to successfully build trust and
empowerment within their teams. In addition, we have found that
strongly believing in the capability of all team members to deliver
excellence, and to hold one another (and ourselves) accountable on
the desired results is a powerful tool to promote both empowerment and engagement.

We have tested different methods, revealed strong results, and
have cascaded those across the enterprise. A few examples of
changes that have taken hold:

➢ Performance discussions are led through the lens of positive
  leadership and include ongoing feedback, coaching, and conversations on accountability.
➢ Guidelines on huddle meetings and other continuous improvement applications have been updated to include recommendations on positive practices to weave into the conversations.
➢ Personal and enterprise purpose is a common discussion topic
  around DTE, and leaders and individual contributors can readily
  share their personal purpose when asked.

Our network has also played a key role in transforming our culture around integrating Force for Growth [FFG; the concept of the company igniting progress in the community] into our everyday work, as there are many overlaps between the tenets of positive leadership and being a force for growth in our communities. At their cores, both efforts include service to others and the understanding that when we do the right thing, the right results will follow. We took a leadership role in integrating FFG into our everyday work and identified key practices to accelerate integration.

Word got out about how we helped with that FFG integration, and we have been invited to help on a few other key projects to help scale transformation across the enterprise. We have helped DTE become a company that is comfortable with innovation, as we have proven through experimentation how to best overcome fear of failure so we can focus on trying new things and creating innovative solutions.

As we have flourished, so has DTE Energy. Engagement is high—we have maxed the Gallup numbers and have identified what "great" looks like in a "post Gallup" world and now use different measurement tools. Through survey feedback, more employees feel like they are welcome to bring their "whole self" to work, and this is supported through advancements in inclusion, opportunities for contribution, and the increased knowledge that DTE Energy cares about what its employees care about.

A bright future: As I walk into this meeting, I am excited to see PEN alumni as well as new members mingling in our premeeting high-quality connection time. Today, we are discussing how we can influence the cultural transformation around innovation, idea management, and recognition of DTE innovators. Each opportunity brings the chance to learn more about myself as a leader, and is a reminder that on this journey, we never stop learning.

I can't wait to see what the year ahead brings!

From Vision to Planning

From the vision statement the people were able to identify a set of potential actions, including the following:

➤ Launch network nodes in their own business units.

➤ Teach other leaders and individual contributors to successfully build trust and empowerment within their teams.

➤ Foster a strong belief in the capability of all team members to deliver excellence, and to hold one another accountable for the desired results.

➤ Lead performance management discussions through the lens of positive leadership and include ongoing feedback, coaching, and conversations on accountability.

➤ Update guidelines on huddle meetings and other CI applications to include recommendations on positive practices to weave into the conversations.

➤ Make personal and team purpose a common discussion topic around DTE, and encourage leaders and individual contributors to readily share their personal purpose when asked.

➤ Take a leadership role in integrating FFG into our everyday work and identify key practices to accelerate integration.

➤ Make recommendations on how to address fear of failure so that it is not seen as a loss but as an integral part of the learning process.

➤ Make more employees feel like they are welcome to bring their "whole self" to work.

See the Appendix to this chapter for more goals set by the positive energizers.

Summary

The idea of positive energizers who can facilitate the embrace of higher purpose throughout the organization is not considered in the traditional principal–agent model because emotion has no role to play in the model. In reality positive energizers, people whose emotional makeup makes them natural change leaders, can be found in every organization. When identified, linked, and empowered, these people will do things senior leaders would never think to ask. Thus, the eighth counterintuitive step in creating a purpose-driven organization is to unleash these positive energizers.

Getting Started: Tools and Exercises

Hold a discussion and structure it as follows:

Phase 1. Have everyone read the chapter and ask them to pay particular attention to the case of the woman who created the network of positive energizers, and to the case of creating the positive energizer network at DTE.

Phase 2. Have everyone write answers to these questions:

➢ What were the key elements in the evolution of the positive energizer network in the first case?

➢ What principles from the first case should we examine for possible application in our organization?

➢ What were the key elements in the evolution of the positive energizer network at DTE?

➢ What principles from the DTE case should we examine for possible application in our organization?

Phase 3. Based on the above discussion create a set of guidelines for identifying, assembling, developing, and nurturing a network of positive energizers in your organization.

Appendix to Chapter 14

1. Using the above list, the members of the positive energizer network (PEN) created a more expansive set of goals. To be a company of higher purpose and to create a more positive culture, they desired to increase the positive practices throughout the enterprise and recognized that they needed to increase trust, encourage empowerment, foster accountability, and move toward their stated aspiration. To accomplish these things they set the following goals.

   a. Personal Development

      i. Commitment by each PEN team member to one personal positive leadership goal in January–February 2018 that they carry out throughout the year in order to serve as a role model for other leaders and team members

      ii. Each PEN member has an accountability partner within PEN to support each other in completing this goal

   b. Enterprise Development

      i. Creation of 8 to 10 nodes in different business units to increase the number of employees implementing positive practices; nodes created by June 1, hold a minimum of three meetings prior to end of 2018

      ii. Creation of report-out template in February 2018 for PEN members to use with their executives to build understanding and easy reference to ensure the top levels of the organization have full understanding of the work and how it benefits DTE

      iii. Attendance of 10 to 15 PEN members at the Positive Business Conference in May 2018 who will share three key learnings with their executive and with their teams/nodes; addition of these learnings to Positive Practice library for C3

      iv. Introduction of PEN and positive practices at 8 to 10 PEN members' all-hands meetings throughout 2018

      v. Completion of 7 to 10 positive leadership/positive practice "lunch and learns" for PEN members' teams throughout 2018

2. Create deeper specificity and understanding of the gaps being addressed by PEN through the following actions:

    a. Enterprise Development

      i. Focus group interviews on the topics of Trust & Empowerment, Purpose, Innovation & Addressing Fear of Failure, and Accountability & Excellence held and analyzed in spring 2018

      ii. Creation of "From/To" documentation for the enterprise and each of the subgroup topics that identifies specific gaps and is finalized by June 1, 2018

      iii. Building out of next-step action plan based on findings to best address gaps throughout the remainder of 2018 and into 2019

3. Solve a business issue through the application of positive practices as they relate to each subgroup topic (Trust & Empowerment, Purpose, Innovation & Addressing Fear of Failure, and Accountability & Excellence). This will be accomplished through the following actions:

    a. By March 15, each subgroup:

      i. Identifies a single challenge that is affecting one member's team or department

      ii. Articulates the gap and the desired outcome

      iii. Brainstorms strategies around their topic (e.g., increasing trust among team members)

    iv. Selects the appropriate course of action to countermeasure the gap

  b. At the March 20 PEN team meeting, each subgroup will report out on their challenge and proposed strategy and will receive feedback from the larger team

  c. After the March 20 meeting, subgroup team members will begin their experiment, and will document the outcomes and share with the larger PEN team at the September 12 PEN meeting

4. Bring growth mind-set to DTE through methods that are inclusive of all 10,000 employees, and will create energy and possibilities throughout the enterprise, through the following actions:

  a. Personal Development

    i. Each PEN member reads the book *Mindset,* by Carol Dweck, by April 1, 2018

    ii. For a one-week period in April or May, each PEN member completes the activity of identifying examples of fixed mind-set in their day-to-day work, documenting ideas on how to transform examples into growth mind-set approach

    iii. Through this exercise, PEN members build their expertise in understanding and identifying growth mind-set opportunities, and can teach and coach other leaders in the organization

    iv. PEN members will share insights on exercise outcomes at May 15 meeting

  b. Enterprise Development

    i. Serve as Growth Mindset ambassadors at July Triannual (specific actions TBD)

    ii. Make recommendations by TBD date to appropriate priority committee to remove organizational roadblocks that hinder growth mind-set approaches (e.g., policies and processes)

    iii. Coach members of their PEN node on growth mind-set before and after July Triannual

    iv. Other actions as determined by PEN members

In our last visit with DTE leaders, they were effusive in their description of the positive energizer network. The network was fully engaged and most goals were being pursued with passion. They are doing things that senior people would have never thought to ask.

CHAPTER FIFTEEN

Taking Action: Answers to Frequently Asked Questions

In this book we put forward an economic theory of higher purpose and eight counterintuitive guidelines for creating a purpose-driven organization. In chapters 7 through 14 we offer exercises or tools that will help you get started. As we have pointed out, most executives avoid purpose work because they are unwilling to engage in something they do not believe in. Purpose work requires a transformation of conventional beliefs.

In this chapter we answer key inquiries that we have gotten from practicing professionals. The answers can allay some of your concerns and help you commit to taking action. The questions fall into three categories: the nature of higher purpose, the economics of higher purpose, and the creation of the purpose-driven organization.

Frequently Asked Questions

The Nature of Higher Purpose

Q: **What is a higher purpose, and how does it influence an individual?**

A: Higher purpose is an authentic or sincere intention to serve
the collective good.

It is the highest contribution you intend to make. Because
you are doing the most significant thing that you can do, the
outcomes matter. By pursuing and producing the outcomes,
you create a sense of meaning. Your highest purpose becomes
your calling. You find intrinsic motivation in the purpose. You
are less influenced by external rewards and punishments.

You pursue higher purpose with full engagement or love.
When you pursue an intention with confident aspiration, you
tend to accelerate learning and perform at a higher level. When
you pursue a purpose with full engagement, you tend to create
excellence, and the process reveals a new self; that self has
more integrity, and a new system of deepened virtues. With
this emergent, virtuous self, you gain genuine self-respect, and
you gain a more positive orientation to others.

Q: **Where does higher purpose come from?**

A: Your personal higher purpose comes from your deepest
motivation to make a contribution to society, so it is connected
to the work you do. Similarly, organizational higher purpose
comes from the deepest motivations of the people in the
organization to make a prosocial contribution, so it is connected
to the business the organization is in. You discover higher
purpose through deep reflection, reflection that occurs outside
the norms. This kind of reflection is work, and it is a form of
labor that everyone tends to resist. Such reflection to discover
your personal higher purpose is typically driven by personal
crisis and leads to the discovery of a new identity and destiny.

Your life narrative is your theory of self. In a crisis, your
narrative is disrupted. By disciplined reflection you can
repair and enhance the narrative. You can achieve the same
end through the choice to engage in daily, disciplined self-

reflection. In doing such work, you renew and enhance your life narrative in small episodes.

Q: **How does organizational higher purpose compare to personal higher purpose?**

A: Like personal higher purpose, organizational higher purpose often comes from crisis. It can, however, come from some form of collective reflection. The organization must tap the deep feeling of multiple actors and integrate their needs in a collective statement.

Q: **How do you find a higher purpose?**

A: You do not invent a higher purpose; you discover it. The discovery requires hard work in the subjective realm. Leaders must come to know and understand the deepest needs and interests of the workforce and customers or clients. For insights on how to discover and articulate a higher purpose, see chapter 8.

Q: **Is higher purpose something you actually achieve, like an objective?**

A: No. Higher purpose is an aspiration that, like the North Star, provides stable direction and guides contribution over time. If your higher purpose is "to inspire positive change," you seek to do that in every situation. You may fully succeed in one situation and not at all in another, but you look to the purpose in every situation. The same is true for the organization. The organization looks to the purpose as its North Star to guide it every step of the journey.

Q: **Does higher purpose change over time?**

A: The world is constantly changing. Individuals and organizations must always be adapting. When an individual or organization follows their higher purpose, they move forward into uncertainty while engaged in deep learning. They produce valued contributions and attract valuable resources. They go through a dynamic learning process.

As purpose-driven people and purpose-driven organizations move forward, they continue to reflect. As a result, they occasionally come to increased clarity and they modify their higher purpose. The change may be large or small, but if it is authentic, the people begin to respond.

Q: How do you sustain higher purpose?

A: When you pursue higher purpose, you achieve profound learning and contribution. From these outcomes you get intrinsic satisfaction and a desire to produce more of the same. You create a self-referential, virtuous cycle. The cycle sustains itself, yet the cycle is fragile. If you fail to monitor and nurture the cycle, it collapses. You must continually integrate reflection and action.

Q. Can you have more than one higher purpose?

A: At the individual level, you might conclude that you have two higher purposes, one at work and one in your personal life. The two statements can be powerful aids. In such a case, you have moved many steps toward finding your higher purpose. Yet one challenge remains. When you find your highest purpose, it integrates all aspects of your life, and it is the arbiter of all decisions. You must often take time and patience to connect with it. For the organization, it may have more than one higher purpose as well, but these must reinforce each other. For example, Zingerman's higher purposes of serving its customers and training its employees to be future entrepreneurs reinforce each other, and create employee engagement and customer satisfaction.

Q: **Why do you emphasize *authentic* higher purpose?**

A: The word *authentic* is perhaps the most important word in
this book. People who make the conventional assumptions
about hierarchical economic life cannot conceive of the notion
of authenticity. Many of them cannot imagine what authentic
communication looks like. An authentic person lives in
integrity with congruence of heart and mind. When managers
become leaders, they become more authentic and more
purposive.

When a higher purpose is inauthentic, it destroys trust and
collaboration. When higher purpose is approached as a tool in
a transactional game, the employees immediately recognize
the hypocrisy. They become more cynical and the managerial
mind has done harm to the organization.

Avoid purpose work if you cannot elevate yourself
into the state of authenticity. For help with this issue, we
recommend the book *Lift: How to Live in the Fundamental
State of Leadership*.[63] (There is also a digital course available.
See "Becoming Who You Really Are: How to Grow
Yourself and Your Organization," Michigan Ross, https://
michiganross.umich.edu/programs/executive-education/
becoming-who-you-really-are-how-grow-yourself-and-your
-organization?event=4147.)

Q: **Is higher purpose related to spirituality?**

A: Researchers who study spirituality struggle to agree on a
definition. Yet one element of the definition is commonly
accepted and is captured in the statement "I feel like I am part
of something bigger than myself."

People who have spiritual experiences tend to describe them
as "oceanic." They have a feeling of being part of one great whole.
Theists often have experiences that involve God, yet atheists may

have such experiences in nature, music, or some other realm. In an organization, higher purpose often leads to trust, bonding, collaboration, collective intelligence, and the co-creation of the future—characteristics of a purpose-driven organization (PDO). In such an organization people may often feel part of one great whole and may have experiences that are spiritual.

The Economics of Higher Purpose

Q: **What is the "economics" of higher purpose?**

A: The "economics" of higher purpose refers to the premise that higher purpose is not charity, something detached from the main business of the organization. The economics of higher purpose is intimately connected to the business of the organization. Indeed, because higher purpose is the arbiter of all business decisions, we focus on the intersection of higher purpose and business purpose. Consequently, it affects employee behavior and business decisions, and the pursuit of higher purpose has economic consequences.

Q: **Why do we need an economics of higher purpose now?**

A: Surveys suggest that younger employees are deeply interested in higher purpose. They want to find meaning in their work. Customers want to buy products that represent fair value and inherent goodness. Investors are slowly beginning to see the emerging demand for organizations of higher purpose. The movement has developed slowly but is now reaching a tipping point. The demand to create PDOs is growing and will soon become intense. If companies do not adopt authentic higher purpose, dissatisfaction with capitalism will grow, and our whole economic way of life will be threatened.

Q: **What is wrong with conventional economics?**

A: Nothing is wrong with conventional economics. Conventional economics is based on sound principles of self-interest, and it produces a clear objective function for firms. In a PDO it is complemented by higher purpose, which provides a powerful way to incentivize employees to behave like purpose-driven leaders and owners who subjugate self-interest to the common good without explicit monetary incentives to do so. In a PDO the contracting frictions and consequent losses of value in the principal–agent framework are reduced.

Q: **If you pursue a higher purpose, can you optimize profits?**

A: Yes. You can find the intersection of business goals— maximizing profits and shareholder value—with the pursuit of higher purpose.

Q: **What are the economic payoffs for creating a PDO?**

A: When higher purpose is authentic—pursued without the expectation of economic gain—and clearly and constantly communicated to the organization, it positively affects not only operating measures of performance like profits and cash flows but also forward-looking measures like stock prices.

Q: **What does higher purpose have to do with capitalism and socialism?**

A: A recent Gallup survey showed that a majority of millennials, for the first time in the history of the survey, favor socialism over capitalism.[64] Millennials feel that way because they have seen the dark side of capitalism—unethical behavior, fines, bailouts of failing companies at taxpayers' expense, and so on—but the prosocial contributions of companies in the capitalistic system are not as evident. They become disillusioned with capitalism, in part because the alternative—

socialism—is viewed as utopia. For capitalism to recapture the hearts and minds of the young, companies must not only embrace authentic higher purpose but also make their pursuit of higher purpose visible and salient.

Q: **How does higher purpose manifest internally versus externally?**

A: Internally, higher purpose energizes employees because they feel they are part of something bigger than themselves. Externally, it attracts customers and others who like to associate with the higher purpose.

Q: **If higher purpose is so impactful, why do so few organizations embrace it and create it?**

A: Organizations have qualms about adopting a higher purpose because embedded deep in the heart of higher purpose is a fundamental economic paradox. Higher purpose produces positive long-term economic gain, but only if it is *not* undertaken with the objective of harvesting that economic gain. Organizations are reluctant to pursue something without the intention of generating profit. Doing so goes against so much of what managers are taught in business schools and in the practical school of experience.

Q: **How will investors react to the idea of higher purpose?**

A: Stakeholders will respond according to their assumptions and beliefs. Narrow economic thinkers will be skeptical. They will be offended unless you can inspire them to a new level of understanding. Here, authenticity plays a key role. If higher purpose is a clever technique, a trick to be played, you will lack the capability to persuade and inspire stakeholders. If purpose is a genuine endeavor, you will become increasingly capable, and external stakeholders will be drawn to the discovery and the embrace of higher purpose. Note that purpose is becoming familiar to the community of investors, and the idea will continue to spread. A tipping point will likely be reached when higher purpose will become a requirement of investors.

Q: **What metrics reflect the success of higher purpose?**

A: Higher purpose should never be measured with the usual economic indicators of success. It should be assessed based on whether it is truly the arbiter of all business decisions.

Creating Purpose-Driven Organizations

Q: **What is a PDO?**

A: A purpose-driven organization is a social system that pursues a higher purpose. The organization takes the purpose as its guiding principle. The PDO pursues a purpose that is authentic and shared because the purpose intersects strategy and is the arbiter of every decision. It has a purpose-driven culture that serves to both stabilize and inspire the people. It is able to transcend the tension represented by the principal–agent problem in economics, or the self-interested behavior of the worker, and every person becomes a principal. It has an engaged workforce that is composed of people bringing their discretionary energy to their work.

Q: **How do PDOs come into being?**

A: Typically, an individual makes the personal journey from manager to leader. This leader begins to live a more proactive and intrinsically driven life. The leader is more fully aware of their own potential or growth, and transcends the conventional mind-set. The leader begins to inspire other people to see and to behave in new ways. As the social network begins to behave

in innovative ways, the people, together, co-create a new
culture and a new organization.

Q: **What turns a manager into a leader of a PDO?**

A: Through crisis or through disciplined self-reflection, the
manager goes through deep change and acquires a new
identity and destiny. The person becomes driven more by
conscience than by culture. They take on new desires and
increased sense of purpose, integrity, courage, authenticity,
empathy, humility, and other virtues. They manifest these
individual virtues, and their positive emotions become
contagious. They become a positive social virus.

Q: **How do you communicate a higher purpose?**

A: Since an authentic higher purpose is the arbiter of all
decisions, the leaders, the middle managers, and the first-line
people communicate the higher purpose with every act. They
act in often unconventional ways, so everyone recognizes
the purpose is authentic, and they take it seriously. They
launch new initiatives at every level. They start a viral process
that gives rise to a new order. They do not dictate the new
order from the top but allow it to be co-created by everyone
engaging in authentic communication. For insights about the
communication of higher purpose see chapters 9, 10, and 13.

Q: **How can you have a PDO when you have diverse departments
and people?**

A: Organizations have a key need to integrate diversity, be it
departmental differences or diversity based on discipline,
status, gender, race, or nationality. Managers cannot integrate
such differentiation. Leaders, on the other hand, are motivated
by virtue rather than ego, they demonstrate genuine concern,
they link people to the future, and they help them think for

themselves. By creating trust and facilitating collaboration, leaders link people and nurture collaboration until the people become wedded to the higher purpose and the diversity is integrated in a unified system of collaborative, collective intelligence.

Q: **How do you create higher purpose in a multinational corporation?**

A: A multinational corporation is a system that crosses geographical boundaries and has employees from different cultures. You might assume that such people have difficulty communicating with one another and that people from different national cultures cannot be easily integrated, The assumption is true; they cannot be easily integrated. They can be integrated through purpose work.

This is the same issue of diversity that we addressed in the last question. The integration of diversity is the work of all leaders. It is difficult work and requires a discovery: all people are unique and all people are the same. Discovering the human commonality is at the heart of purpose work and is a form of deep learning that leaders come to understand and execute.

Q: **How can you take higher purpose to the lower levels of the organization?**

A: You must take higher purpose all the way down the organization. Most executives cannot figure out how to do this, and this is one of the reasons why their efforts to establish higher purpose fail. For insights on how to move the purpose down the organization, see the last three chapters.

Q: **What changes account for the success of organizations that pursue higher purpose?**

A: A PDO transcends the principal–agent problem and alters the social fabric. It changes communication from downloading to honest debate, to authentic dialogue, to emergent collective learning. It allows ideas to be challenged while maintaining respectful relationships. It encourages people to bring their discretionary energy to work.

As individuals change, the collective changes. Negative peer pressure morphs into positive peer pressure. People sacrifice for the common good. Leadership becomes distributed, with people taking spontaneous initiatives. A new order emerges that is aligned with current external realities. Success breeds success, external stakeholders are drawn to the organization, and new resources begin to flow to the organization.

Q: **Can all organizations apply the principles of higher purpose?**

A: People with the conventional mind-set focus on constraints and arguments as to why a given organization cannot be purpose driven. They articulate constraints that are real and formidable. Yet the very purpose of leadership is to transcend conventional constraints and create a PDO. In this book, we give examples from the most technical and hierarchical fields of endeavor. It is difficult to create a PDO in all domains, particularly those where all the emphasis is on transactional contracts and trust is low, but such organizations are the ones that have the most to gain.

One way you can begin envisioning a PDO is to look for organizations in the same domain that defy logic and operate from higher purpose. We often hear people tell us, "This would never work on Wall Street." Yet Jimmy Dunne is someone on Wall Street who is creating a PDO (see chapter 9). When we point out such cases, people respond, "Oh, that doesn't count," and they search for something about their organization that is different that will excuse them from the accountability of purpose work. We suggest that you examine the end of the normal curve where excellence exists, and there you will find the positive deviance that will help you envision the impossible. Remember, if it is real, it is possible.

Q: **How does company culture influence efforts to find and pursue a higher purpose?**

A: Most companies and organizations have a conventional culture. Cultures function to preserve themselves, and people who propose significant changes are punished. For this reason, change agents must become purpose-driven leaders. Most executives, like the rest of us, are fearful, so most organizations do not become purpose driven. The leader has a calling to create conflict by continually moving the current culture in a more positive direction.

Q: **What if an organization succeeded as a PDO, then failed. Can it be turned around?**

A: Excellence is fragile. Once it is achieved and lost, we tend to assume that the social system will be too injured to recover. Yet in such an organization valuable assets remain, embodied in a working memory of excellence and of decay. By surfacing and examining the two realities, we can explore how we want to live in the organization and then ask ourselves how to create excellence in the present moment.

Q: **What if you believe in having a purpose-driven organization, but the people above you and around you do not?**

A: A person in this situation tends to conclude that nothing can be done. The conclusion is an indication that the actor is still in the conventional, managerial mind-set. But a leader is transformational. A leader transforms the beliefs of those below, at the same level, and above. If this question reflects your perspective, seek to discover your own highest purpose and begin to live from an internal locus of control. Doing so will teach you how to do things you think you cannot do.

Q: **How do you find the time and energy to create a PDO?**

A: The conventional manager lives a reactive, fear-filled life that is short on meaning. The conventional manager cannot find the time or energy to reflect and has limited options for renewal. The purpose-driven leader can find no higher intention than to pursue the highest purpose. Pursuing the purpose paradoxically produces energy and saves time. Purpose-driven leaders are fully engaged.

Q: **If my company is already successful, how does it become a PDO?**

A: The conventional answer is to create a burning platform, some problem that will capture the attention and force commitment. Our answer is create a burning desire. Look around and discover excellence in the real world, understand the excellence, link the excellence to the deepest needs of your people, align yourself with the excellence, become a constant example of the excellence, speak continually of your aspiration, and align all strategies and processes with the excellence. The approach is based on attraction rather than compulsion.

Q: **How do you reconcile the fact that you are a PDO, yet some of your failures are aligned with higher purpose and some of your successes are not aligned with higher purpose?**

A: As this question illustrates, you never fully succeed in creating a PDO. Organizations are complex, and conflicts never stop arising. Some projects naturally evolve away from the purpose. In terms of profit they may even succeed. A purpose-driven initiative may fail. To maintain a PDO you must engage in continuous reflection and evaluate whether every action is driven by purpose. It is a journey filled with failure and continual recovery.

Q: **What if you are in a PDO but you are working on a project that is not aligned with the higher purpose?**

A: This is easy. If you have a PDO and you are working on a project that is not aligned with the higher purpose, you can speak up and challenge the project. Because you are in a PDO, people will openly discuss the issue and come to a consensus that is satisfying to all. If this is not the case, you do not have a PDO.

Q: **What does a higher purpose have to do with finding good talent?**

A: Companies that become purpose-driven evolve a culture of excellence in which people are valued. Such cultures differ from the conventional, transactional cultures that mark most organizations. Talent is attracted to a PDO because employees acquire resources that far exceed their salaries. An organization that becomes a PDO often shows up on a list of best places to work.

Q: **What happens to higher purpose after it brings an organization economic success?**

A: If the purpose is authentic, the answer is that nothing happens. If the organization is seduced by economic success without purpose, leadership has work to do.

Q: **If you create a PDO, how do you sustain it?**

A: An organization is a dynamic system, and when an organization becomes a PDO, human nature works to undermine it. A PDO is sustained by leaders who continually focus on the repair and enhancement of the culture. That focus is the difference between a manager and a leader. The manager thinks only of strategy; the leader thinks of culture and strategy as one dynamic system that needs to be constantly knitted together.

Some Final Advice

The conventional mind-set opposes the concept of higher purpose, people of higher purpose threaten the existing culture, and most executives shun purpose work. For you this is an opportunity. If you are willing to become a purpose-driven leader and implement the eight steps to organizational change detailed in this book, you will evolve into a new person, a leader rather than a manager. You will be a leader who looks at the principal–agent problem and sees the principal–agent opportunity, a leader who turns agents into principals.

In your journey to purpose attend to the word *authenticity*. You do not seek a higher purpose to satisfy external demands. You do it because you believe in it, because you are convinced that higher purpose energizes people and elevates the organization. Higher purpose stabilizes the organization as self-interest is sacrificed for the common good. Then the collective interest and the self-interest become one. People bring their creative energy to work like never before. *The time being taken away from the here and now to do purpose work is actually an investment in radically transforming the here and now.*

Begin by reflecting on the eight steps to organizational change that we have shared here. Remember that the first step is a change in your own mind-set. *You* must believe that your organization can be transformed into a purpose-driven organization with a purpose-driven workforce. And, above all, you must be genuine in your purpose and clear in your communication of that purpose. If you do that, you will leave a legacy behind that will long outlive you. Significance *is* success.

NOTES

Chapter One: Seeing What Cannot Be Seen

1. Micah Solomon, "5 Wow Customer Service Stories from 5-Star Hotels: Examples Any Business Can Learn From," *Forbes*, July 29, 2017.

2. Joan Magretta, "Growth Through Global Sustainability: An Interview with Monsanto's CEO, Robert B. Shapiro," *Harvard Business Review*, January/February 1997.

3. P. A. David, "Path Dependence, a Foundational Concept for Historical Social Science," *Cliometrica* 1, no. 2 (2007): 91–114.

Chapter Two: Higher Purpose Changes Everything

4. This account is adapted from R. E. Quinn and G. T. Quinn, *Letters to Garrett: Stories of Change, Power and Possibility* (San Francisco: Jossey Bass, 2002), chapter 2.

5. B. Fredrickson, *Positivity* (New York: Crown Publishers, 2009), chapter 9.

6. R. W. Quinn and R. E. Quinn, *Lift: The Fundamental State of Leadership* (Oakland, CA: Berrett-Koehler, 2015), chapters 3 and 4.

7. V. J. Strecher, *Life on Purpose: How Living for What Matters Most Changes Everything* (New York: Harper One, 2016), chapter 1.

8. On adding years, see P. L. Hill and N. A. Turiano, "Purpose in Life as a Predictor of Mortality Across Adulthood," *Psychological Science* 25, no 7 (2014): 1482–86; on heart attack and stroke, see E. S. Kim et al., "Purpose in Life and Reduced Risk of Myocardial Infarction Among Older US Adults with Coronary Heart Disease: A Two-Year Follow-Up," *Journal of Behavioral Medicine*, February 2012; on Alzheimer's disease, see P. A. Boyle et al., "Effect of a Purpose in Life on Risk of Incident Alzheimer Disease and Mild Cognitive Impairment in Community Dwelling Older Persons," *Archives of General Psychiatry* 67, no. 3 (2010):

304–10; on sexual enjoyment, see B. A. Prairie et al., "A Higher Sense of Purpose in Life Is Associated with Sexual Enjoyment in Midlife Women," *Menopause* 18, no. 8 (2011): 839–44; on sleep, see E. S. Kim, S. D. Hershner, and V. J. Strecher, "Purpose in Life and Incidence of Sleep Disturbances," *Journal of Behavior Medicine* 38, no. 3 (2015): 590–97; on depression, see A. M. Wood and S. Joseph, "The Absence of Positive Psychological (Eudemonic) Well-Being as a Risk Factor for Depression: A Ten-Year Cohort Study," *Journal of Affective Disorders* 122 (2010): 213–17; on drugs and alcohol, see R. A. Martin et al., "Purpose in Life Predicts Treatment Outcomes Among Adult Cocaine Abusers in Treatment," *Journal of Substance Abuse Treatment* 40, no 2 (2011): 183–188; on killer cells, see B. L. Fredrickson et al., "A Functional Genomic Perspective on Human Well-Being," *Proceeding of the National Academy of Science* 110 (2013): 13684–89; on cholesterol, see C. D. Ryff, B. Singer, and G. D. Love, "Positive Health: Connection Well-Being with Biology," *Philosophical Transactions of the Royal Society of London: Biological Sciences* 359 (2004): 1383–94; on performance, see A. M. Grant and J. M. Berg, "Prosocial Motivation at Work: When, Why, and How Making a Difference Makes a Difference," in *The Oxford Handbook of Positive Organizational Scholarship*, eds. K. S. Cameron and G. M. Spreitzer (New York: Oxford University Press, 2012), 28–44.

9. See Manju Puri and David Robinson, "Optimism and Economic Choice," *Journal of Financial Economics*, 2007.

10. *The Human Era @ Work: Findings from the Energy Project and Harvard Business Review, 2014*, https://uli.org/wp-content/uploads/ULI -Documents/The-Human-Era-at-Work.pdf.

11. Irrigation Association, "Shark Tank Success Story to Appear at 2017 Irrigation Show and Education Conference," press release, September 11, 2017, https://www.irrigation.org/IA/News/Press-Releases -Folder/SharkTanksuccessstorytoappearat2017IrrigationShowEducation Conference.aspx.

Chapter Three: Imagining Organizations of Higher Purpose

12. This account is adapted from R. E. Quinn, *The Positive Organization: Breaking Free from Conventional Cultures, Constraints, and Beliefs* (Oakland, CA: Berrett-Koehler, 2015), chapter 2.

13. A. L. Molinsky, A. M. Grant, and J. D. Margolis, "The Bedside

Manner of Homo Economicus: How and Why Priming an Economic Schema Reduces Compassion," *Organizational Behavior and Human Decision Processes* 119, no. 1: 27–37.

14. Some economists have recognized the weaknesses of high-powered incentives in "multitasking environments" to explain why some organizations choose not to use high-powered incentives that focus on easily identified economic outcomes. See, for example, Bengt Holmstrom and Paul Milgrom, "Multitask Principal–Agent Analyses: Incentive Contracts, Asset Ownership, and Job Design," *Journal of Law, Economics, & Organization* in special issue: Papers from the Conference on the New Science of Organization 7 (1991): 24–52.

15. Indeed, recent research in economics has focused on economic theories of corporate culture and trust. See, for example, Song Fenghua and Anjan Thakor, "Bank Culture," *Journal of Financial Intermediation* (forthcoming, 2019). For an economic theory of trust, see Richard Thakor and Robert Merton, "Trust in Lending," MIT Sloan Working Paper, March 2019.

Chapter Four: Transforming Self-interest

16. See James Mirrlees, "The Optimal Structure of Authority and Incentives Within the Organization," *Bell Journal of Economics* 7, no. 1 (February 1976): 105–31; and Bengt Holmstrom, "Moral Hazard and Observability," *Bell Journal of Economics* 10, no. 1: 74–91.

17. See Candice Prendergrast, "The Tenuous Tradeoff Between Risk and Incentives," *Journal of Political Economy* 110, no. 5 (October 2002): 1071–1102.

18. See National Academy of Sciences, Health and Medicine Division, "Best Care at Lower Cost: The Path to Continuously Learning Health Care in America," news release, September 6, 2012.

19. See Eva A. Kerr and John Z. Avanian, "How to Stop the Overconsumption of Health Care," *Harvard Business Review*, October 1, 2014.

20. See Edward Lazear, "Performance Pay and Productivity" (NBER Working Paper No. 5672, National Bureau of Economic Research, Cambridge, MA). About half of this productivity increase came from a "selection effect," wherein the most able workers were attracted to piece rates and the less able workers left.

21. H. Paarsch and B. Paarsch, "Fixed Wages, Piece Rates, and Incentive Effects" (mimeograph, University of Laval, Quebec, 1996).

22. See S. Fernie and D. Metcalf, "It's Not What You Pay, It's the Way You Pay It and That's What Gets Results: Jockeys' Pay for Performance" (mimeograph, London School of Economics, 1996). For a review of this literature, see Canice Prendergast, "What Happens Within Firms? A Survey of Empirical Evidence on Compensation Policies," in *Labor Statistics Measurement Issues*, eds. John Haltiwanger, Marilyn Manser, and Robert Topel (Chicago: University of Chicago Press, 1998).

23. See George Baker, Michael Jensen, and Kevin Murphy, "Compensation and Incentives: Practice Versus Theory," *Journal of Finance* 43, no. 3 (July 1988): 593–616.

24. See Anjan V. Thakor, "Corporate Culture in Banking," *Federal Reserve Bank of New York Policy Review*, August 2016, 1–16 .

25. See Oege Dijk and Martin Holmen, "Charity, Incentives and Performance" (working paper, University of Gothenburg, November 2012).

26. On society, integrity, honesty, social identity, and reputation, see George Akerlof and Rachel Kranton, "Identity Economics: How Our Identities Shape Our Work, Wages and Well Being," *Public Choice* 145 no. 1/2 (October 2010): 325–28; on corporate social responsibility, see Roland Benabou and Jean Tirole, "Individual and Corporate Social Responsibility," *Economica* 77, no. 305 (January 2010): 1–19; on moral behavior, see Roland Benabou and Jean Tirole, "Identity, Morals, and Taboos: Beliefs as Assets," *The Quarterly Journal of Economics* 126, no. 2 (May 2011): 805–55; on intrinsic motivation, see Roland Benabou and Jean Tirole, "Intrinsic and Extrinsic Motivation," *The Review of Economic Studies* 70, no. 3 (July 2003): 489–520.

Chapter Five: Reframing Economics

27. See John Sculley, "John Sculley on Steve Jobs," *Bloomberg Businessweek*, October 10, 2011.

28. In other words, we are not studying charitable foundations like the Bill and Melinda Gates Foundation.

29. This quotation was part of Walt Disney's pitch to Wall Street while seeking funding to build Disneyland.

30. Richard J. Leider, *The Power of Purpose* (San Francisco: Berrett-Koehler, 1997).

31. See Kenneth E. Boulding, "Economics as a Moral Science," *American Economic Review* 59, no. 1, 1969: 1–12.

32. See A. M. Grant and J. M. Berg, "Prosocial Motivation at Work: When, Why, and How Making a Difference Makes a Difference," in *The Oxford Handbook of Positive Organizational Scholarship*, eds. K. S. Cameron and G. M. Spreitzer (New York: Oxford University Press, 2012), 28–44.

33. Walt Disney, quoted in Bob Thomas, *Walt Disney: An American Original* (New York: Simon and Schuster, 1976), 246–47.

34. See Benjamin E. Hermalin, "Toward an Economic Theory of Leadership: Leading by Example," *American Economic Review* 88, no. 5 (December 1998): 1088–1120. This paper proposes that effective leadership involves a personal sacrifice for the common good.

35. K. S. Cameron, *Practicing Positive Leadership* (Oakland, CA: Berrett-Koehler, 2013), 11–13.

36. Cameron, *Practicing Positive Leadership*, 11–13.

37. Conor Shine, "Southwest's Heavy Heart: How the LUV Airline Is Responding to the Worst Accident in Its History," *Dallas News*, April 22, 2018.

38. Oege Dijk and Martin Holmen, "Charity, Incentives and Performance" (working paper, University of Gothenburg, November 2012). The authors refer to the donation of earnings to the Swedish Red Cross in their experiment not as pursuing higher purpose but rather as "charity." However, the decision of participants to give to the Red Cross from earnings generates effects on agents (employees) that are similar to those of our economic theory of higher purpose.

39. Claudine Gartenberg, Andrea Prat, and George Serafeim, "Corporate Purpose and Financial Performance," *Organization Science* 30 (1), January–February 2019, 1–18.

40. H. Dai and D. Zhang, "Prosocial Goal Pursuit Outweighs Herding in Crowdfunding: Evidence from Kickstarter.com," *Journal of Marketing Research* (forthcoming), https://papers.ssrn.com/so13/papers.cfm?abstract_id=2954217.

41. Rui Abuquerque, Yjro Koskinen, and Chendi Zhang, "Corporate Social Responsibility and Firm Risk: Theory and Empirical Evidence," *Management Science* (forthcoming).

Chapter Six: Why Isn't Everyone Doing It?

42. See the discussion of this issue in Robert Kaplan, George Serafeim, and Eduardo Tugendhat, "Inclusive Growth: Profitable Strategies for Tackling Poverty and Inequality," *Harvard Business Review*, January–February 2018, 128–33.

43. See Frank Newport, "Democrats More Positive About Socialism than Capitalism," *Gallup*, August 13, 2018.

44. Indeed, the more people believe that companies are adopting higher purpose to bow to pressures from regulators or politicians, the less authentic those adoptions will appear and the less effective they will be in changing behavior.

45. Kaplan, Serafeim, and Tugendhat, "Inclusive Growth."

46. Economists refer to these as "private benefit projects." See, for example, Bengt Holmstrom and Jean Tirole, "Financial Intermediation, Loanable Funds, and the Real Sector," *Quarterly Journal of Economics* 112–13 (August 1997), 663–91.

47. V. J. Strecher, *Life on Purpose: How Living for What Matters Most Changes Everything* (New York: Harper One, 2016).

Chapter Seven: `STEP 1` Envision the Purpose-Driven Organization

48. This example is taken from R. E. Quinn and A. J. Thakor, "Creating a Purpose-Driven Organization: How to Get Employees to Bring Their Smarts and Their Energy to Work," *Harvard Business Review*, July–August, 2018: 78–85.

Chapter Eight: `STEP 2` Discover the Purpose

49. E. Easwaran, *Timeless Wisdom: Passages for Meditation from the World's Saints and Sages* (Tomales, CA: Blue Mountain Center for Meditation, 2008), 20.

50. N. Craig, *Leading from Purpose: Clarity and Confidence to Act When It Matters Most* (New York: Hachette Books, 2018).

51. R. W. Quinn and R. E. Quinn, *Lift: The Fundamental State of Leadership* (Oakland, CA: Berrett-Koehler, 2015), chapters 3 and 4.

52. Craig, *Leading from Purpose*, chapter 15.

Chapter Nine: **STEP 3** Meet the Need for Authenticity

53. Recall our discussion of pet projects in chapter 6. The manipulator does not maximize the value of the firm and sees the organization as a collection of manipulators rather than authentic leaders. Given this assumption, the manipulator behaves in a way that elicits behavior from others that validates his assumption about them!

Chapter Eleven: **STEP 5** Stimulate Learning

54. A. M. Grant and J. M. Berg, "Prosocial Motivation at Work: When, Why, and How Making a Difference Makes a Difference," in *The Oxford Handbook of Positive Organizational Scholarship*, eds. K. S. Cameron and G. M. Spreitzer (New York: Oxford University Press, 2012), 28–44.

55. C. Dweck, *Mindset: The New Psychology of Success* (New York: Ballantine, 2016).

56. J. K. Harter and N. Blacksmith, "Employee Engagement and the Psychology of Joining, Staying In, and Leaving Organizations," in *Oxford Handbook of Positive Psychology and Work* (New York: Oxford University Press, 2010), 121–30.

57. Harter and Blacksmith, "Employee Engagement and the Psychology of Joining, Staying In, and Leaving Organizations."

58. A. Weinzweig, *A Lapsed Anarchist's Approach to Building a Great Business* (Ann Arbor, MI: Zingerman's Press, 2010), 316–24.

Chapter Twelve: **STEP 6** Turn Midlevel Managers into Purpose-Driven Leaders

59. A. J. Thakor and R. E. Quinn, "The Economics of Higher Purpose," *Harvard Business Review*, July–August 2018.

Chapter Thirteen: **STEP 7** Connect the People to the Purpose

60. N. Fernandez, "In the First Person—Ray Anderson, Chairman and CEO of Interface Inc.," in *Earth Care: An Anthology in Environmental Ethics*, eds. D. Clowney and P. Mosto (New York: Bowman and Littlefield Publishers, 2009), 704.

61. A. J. Thakor and R. E. Quinn, "The Economics of Higher Purpose," *Harvard Business Review*, July–August 2018.

62. K. S. Cameron, J. E. Dutton, and R. E. Quinn, *Positive Organizational Scholarship: Foundations of a New Discipline* (San Francisco: Berrett-Koehler Publishers, 2003).

Chapter Fifteen: Taking Action: Answers to Frequently Asked Questions

63. R. W. Quinn and R. E. Quinn, *Lift: How to Live in a Fundamental State of Leadership* (Oakland, CA: Berrett-Koehler, 2015).
64. See Frank Newport, "Democrats More Favorable About Socialism Than Capitalism," *Gallup*, August 13, 2018.

ACKNOWLEDGMENTS

In a workshop with executives discussing purpose in life and work, one of the participants shared a story. In his first career, he was a chef. An angry teenager was a dishwasher there. The chef told the teenager he was going to teach him how to make his secret ravioli recipe, and he had the teenager make the dish each day. One day, he told him that he was the only person on the planet who knew how to do what he was doing.

The chef's teaching had an impact on the teenager, who began to grow. He went into the military and fought in two wars. Twenty-five years later, he found the chef on Facebook and thanked him for turning his life around.

The former chef said, "I continually search for ways to help people grow. This is why I work. Money is necessary to live, but this is my most important form of pay. It is my reason to live."

The room grew silent. Another participant spoke up: "Thank you for sharing that story; it really matters to me."

We want this book to help people grow. We want to have the message really matter to you.

In order to write this book, we invited people to help us grow, and we live in gratitude to them. We are thankful for our immediate colleagues who have shaped our thinking, including Horst Abraham, Sue Ashford, Wayne Baker, Kim Cameron, Jeff DeGraff, Jane Dutton, Shirli Kopelman, Dave Mayer, Ryan Quinn, Shawn Quinn, Nina Ramsey, Gretchen Spreitzer, Vic Strecher, Jim Walsh, and Amy Young.

We are deeply indebted to the many extraordinary people who

shared their stories, including Gerry Anderson, Deborah Ball, Amy Byron-Oiler, Nick Craig, Jimmy Dunne, Eric Greitens, Kathryn Haessler, Jim Haudan, Ricardo Levy, Richard (Dick) Mahoney, Tony Meola, Roger Newton, Shawn Patterson, Bruce Pfau, Shauri Quinn Dewey, Amy Schwartz, Gina Valenti, John Veihmeyer, Jim Weddle, Ari Weinzweig, and Alberto Weisser.

Finally, we are grateful to the wonderful staff at Berrett-Koehler Publishers, especially Steve Piersanti and Jeevan Sivasubramaniam. Berrett-Koehler is an organization of higher purpose, and we always grow when we work with them.

INDEX

Abraham, Horst, 85–86, 88
Anderson, Gerry, 114–116, 121
Anderson, Ray, 156–158
Attentional gravity, 127–128
Attribution bias, 32
Authentic communication, 119–121
  purpose and, 114–116
Authenticity, 13, 14, 111. *See also specific*
  topics
  constancy and, 11, 62, 124, 128, 129
  conventional assumptions about,
    111–112, 124–125
  definition and nature of, 13
  dimensions of, 112
  meeting the need for, 9
  Ricardo Levy and, 47

Ball, Deborah, 100–101
Being state, changing and controlling
  one's, 21
Belief. *See also* True believers
  lack of, 7
Bible, 49–50
"Bilingual leaders," ix, xii
Bottom-up effort, need for, 162
Bottom-up leadership, xiii
Bottom-up process of change, 132, 160
Boulding, Kenneth, 54
Business purpose, 3. *See also specific*
  topics
  higher purpose and, 3, 75, 191
Business strategy, intersection of
  higher purpose and, 25
Byron-Oilar, Amy, 165–167

Capitalism, 191. *See also* Free-market
  capitalism
  higher purpose, socialism, and,
    192–193
Carana Corporation, 71–72

Chapman, Robert, 31
Chief executive officers (CEOs). *See*
  also Executives
  principal–agent model and, 109,
    123, 138, 154
  purpose-driven, 15–16
  reasons they do not pursue higher
    purpose, 7
Chief financial officers (CFOs),
  113–114
Childhood, examining one's magical
  moments in, 103
Childhood stories, 106
Coldren, Jay, 4
Collaboration, xii, xiii, 35–37, 47,
  79–81, 113
  diversity and, 196
  higher purpose and, 158, 190, 191
  Zingerman's and, 140, 142
Collaborative culture, 32, 118
Collaborative relationships, 95
Collective good. *See also under*
  Self-interest
  serving the, 187
Collective identity, 50
Collective intelligence, x, xii
Collective interest. *See under*
  Self-interest
Collective learning, 96
Collective purpose. *See also*
  Organizational purpose
  personal purpose and, 104, 172–175
Communication. *See also* Authentic
  communication; Constantly
  communicating purpose
  how to communicate a higher
    purpose, 195
Community, the covenant and, 49–51
Company culture. *See* Culture
Confrontation, constructive, 96

ABOUT THE AUTHORS

 ROBERT E. QUINN is the Margaret Elliot Tracy Collegiate Professor Emeritus at the University of Michigan's Ross School of Business. He is one of the cofounders of the field of positive organizational scholarship. He has written 18 books. He is in the top 1 percent of professors cited in organizational behavior textbooks. He is the recipient of multiple teaching awards. In a global survey he was recognized as one of the top speakers on the topic of organizational culture and related issues. More than 15 million people viewed his video talk on purpose.

 ANJAN V. THAKOR is the John E. Simon Professor of Finance, Director of the PhD program, and Director of the WFA Center for Finance and Accounting Research in the Olin School of Business at Washington University in St. Louis. He is a research associate of the European Corporate Governance Institute and a Fellow of The Financial Theory Group. He served as managing editor of *Journal of Financial Intermediation* from 1996 to 2005 and currently serves as an associate editor. He is past president and a founder of the Financial Intermediation Research Society. He has published his research extensively in the top economics and finance journals. He has been named as the fourth most prolific researcher in the world in finance over the past 50 years based on

publications in the top seven finance journals over that time, and as one of the five-most prolific finance authors in the world from 2005 to 2015. He has been actively involved in advising PhD students who have gone on to enjoy distinguished academic careers and has chaired dissertation committees of more than 30 students who have received their PhDs. He has won numerous teaching awards in the MBA, Executive MBA, and PhD programs. He has consulted with numerous corporations.

More from Robert E. Quinn

The Positive Organization

Breaking Free from Conventional Cultures, Constraints, and Beliefs

Robert E. Quinn

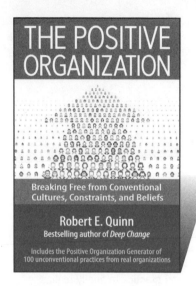

Too many enterprises waste human potential. Robert Quinn shows how to defy convention and create organizations where people feel fully engaged and continually rewarded. The problem is that leaders are following a negative and constraining "mental map" that insists organizations must be rigid, top-down hierarchies and that the people in them are driven mainly by self-interest and fear. But leaders can adopt a different mental map, one where organizations are networks of fluid, evolving relationships and where people are motivated by a desire to grow, learn, and serve a larger goal. Using dozens of memorable stories, Quinn describes specific actions leaders can take to facilitate the emergence of this organizational culture—helping people gain a sense of purpose, engage in authentic conversations, see new possibilities, and sacrifice for the common good.

Hardcover, 168 pages, ISBN 978-1-62656-562-3
PDF ebook, ISBN 978-1-62656-563-0
ePub ebook ISBN 978-1-62656-564-7
Digital audio, ISBN 978-1-62656-745-0

BK® Berrett–Koehler Publishers, Inc.
www.bkconnection.com

800.929.2929

Lift, 2nd edition
The Fundamental State of Leadership
Ryan W. Quinn and Robert E. Quinn

Just as the Wright Brothers combined science and practice to finally realize the dream of flight, Ryan and Robert Quinn combine research and personal experience to demonstrate how to reach a psychological state that lifts us and those around us to greater heights of achievement, integrity, openness, and empathy. The updated edition of this award-winning book—honored by Utah State University's Huntsman School of Business, Benedictine University, and the LeadershipNow web site --includes two new chapters, one describing a learning process and social media platform the Quinns created to help people experience lift and the other sharing new insights into tapping into human potential.

Paperback, 288 pages, ISBN 978-1-62656-401-5
PDF ebook, ISBN 978-1-62656-402-2
ePub ebook ISBN 978-1-62656-403-9
Digital audio, ISBN 978-1-62656-746-7

Berrett–Koehler Publishers, Inc.
www.bkconnection.com

800.929.2929

The Best Teacher in You
How to Accelerate Learning and Change Lives
Robert E. Quinn, Katherine Heynoski, Mike Thomas, and Gretchen M. Spreitzer

What does teaching look like at its very best? How are great teachers able to ignite a love of learning and change students' lives? In this book you'll learn from seven remarkable teachers who stretch beyond the conventional foundations of good teaching to transform their classrooms into exciting, dynamic places where teachers and students cocreate the learning experience. Based on six years of extensive work, the book outlines a framework that identifies four dimensions of effective teaching and learning that are integrated in these highly effective teachers' classrooms—and that all teachers can use to recognize and release the potential in themselves and their students.

Paperback, 240 pages, ISBN 978-1-62656-178-6
PDF ebook, ISBN 978-1-62656-179-3
ePub ebook ISBN 978-1-62656-180-9

Berrett–Koehler Publishers, Inc.
www.bkconnection.com

800.929.2929

Positive Organizational Scholarship
Foundations of a New Discipline
Kim S. Cameron, Jane E. Dutton, and Robert E. Quinn, Editors

Just as positive psychology focuses on exploring optimal individual psychological states rather than pathological ones, *Positive Organizational Scholarship*
focuses attention on optimal organizational states - the dynamics in organizations
that lead to the development of human strength, foster resiliency in employees, make healing, restoration, and reconciliation possible, and cultivate
extraordinary individual and organizational performance. The contributors
of *Positive Organizational Scholarship* rigorously seek to understand what
represents the best of the human condition based on scholarly research and
theory. This book invites organizational scholars to build upon and extend the
positive organizational phenomena being examined. It provides the definition-
al, theoretical, and empirical foundations for what will become a cumulative
body of enduring work.

Hardcover, 480 pages, ISBN 978-1-57675-232-6
PDF ebook, ISBN 978-1-60509-438-0
ePub ebook ISBN 978-1-57675-966-0

Berrett–Koehler Publishers, Inc.
www.bkconnection.com   **800.929.2929**

Berrett–Koehler
Publishers

Berrett-Koehler is an independent publisher dedicated to an ambitious mission: *Connecting people and ideas to create a world that works for all.*

Our publications span many formats, including print, digital, audio, and video. We also offer online resources, training, and gatherings. And we will continue expanding our products and services to advance our mission.

We believe that the solutions to the world's problems will come from all of us, working at all levels: in our society, in our organizations, and in our own lives. Our publications and resources offer pathways to creating a more just, equitable, and sustainable society. They help people make their organizations more humane, democratic, diverse, and effective (and we don't think there's any contradiction there). And they guide people in creating positive change in their own lives and aligning their personal practices with their aspirations for a better world.

And we strive to practice what we preach through what we call "The BK Way." At the core of this approach is *stewardship,* a deep sense of responsibility to administer the company for the benefit of all of our stakeholder groups, including authors, customers, employees, investors, service providers, sales partners, and the communities and environment around us. Everything we do is built around stewardship and our other core values of *quality, partnership, inclusion,* and *sustainability.*

This is why Berrett-Koehler is the first book publishing company to be both a B Corporation (a rigorous certification) and a benefit corporation (a for-profit legal status), which together require us to adhere to the highest standards for corporate, social, and environmental performance. And it is why we have instituted many pioneering practices (which you can learn about at www.bkconnection.com), including the Berrett-Koehler Constitution, the Bill of Rights and Responsibilities for BK Authors, and our unique Author Days.

We are grateful to our readers, authors, and other friends who are supporting our mission. We ask you to share with us examples of how BK publications and resources are making a difference in your lives, organizations, and communities at www.bkconnection.com/impact.

Dear reader,

Thank you for picking up this book and welcome to the worldwide BK community! You're joining a special group of people who have come together to create positive change in their lives, organizations, and communities.

What's BK all about?

Our mission is to connect people and ideas to create a world that works for all.

Why? Our communities, organizations, and lives get bogged down by old paradigms of self-interest, exclusion, hierarchy, and privilege. But we believe that can change. That's why we seek the leading experts on these challenges—and share their actionable ideas with you.

A welcome gift

To help you get started, we'd like to offer you a **free copy** of one of our bestselling ebooks:

www.bkconnection.com/welcome

When you claim your **free ebook**, you'll also be subscribed to our blog.

Our freshest insights

Access the best new tools and ideas for leaders at all levels on our blog at ideas.bkconnection.com.

Sincerely,

Your friends at Berrett-Koehler

Certified

Corporation